Maths Spotlight

Pupil Book

6

Heinemann

| Series editors | Peter Clarke |
| | Len Frobisher |

Writing team	Janine Blinko
	Paula Coombes
	Hilary Koll
	Steve Mills
	Jeanette Mumford

Heinemann is an imprint of Pearson Education Limited, a company incorporated in England and Wales, having its registered office at Edinburgh Gate, Harlow, Essex, CM20 2JE.
Registered company number: 872828
www.heinemann.co.uk

Heinemann is a registered trademark of Pearson Education Ltd

First published 2003

10 09
10, 9, 8, 7, 6

ISBN 978 0 435207 78 6

Illustrated by Andy Hamilton and Derek Matthews
Cover illustration by Dave Cockburn
Cover Design by Paul Goodman
Designed by bigtop, Bicester, UK
Printed and bound in China (CTPS / 06)

Contents

Let's practise

1 Multiply each of these numbers by 100 and 1000.

a 3 **b** 42 **c** 854 **d** 701

e 2·4 **f** 6·31 **g** 0·472 **h** 3·004

2 Divide each of these numbers by 100 and 1000.

a 6532 **b** 394 **c** 83·9 **d** 67·02

e 5 **f** 0·1 **g** 3·1 **h** 7·04

Zero

An Indian textbook, dating from c.200 BCE, contains the first recorded use of zero.

The Roman number system did not use zero at all.

3 Write in words the numbers on these calculators.

a 680720 **b** 680720.4 **c** 6807.204

d 6807204 **e** 68072.04 **f** 680.7204

4 In the skating competition there has been a scoring error.
Add 0·1 to each score.

a 6·2 **b** 7·9 **c** 8·35 **d** 3·76 **e** 9·9

5 There has been another scoring error.
This time subtract 0·01 from each score.

a 8·6 **b** 4·07 **c** 3·0 **d** 8·1 **e** 9·01

Let's play A game for 2

- Player 1 enters a 6-digit number on their calculator.
- Player 2 enters the same 6 digits in the same order on their calculator but places a decimal point between 2 of the digits.
- Player 1 scores a point by dividing once to make their display match player 2's number.

458291

4582.91

The winner is the player with more points after 6 games.

Let's practise

1 Copy and write **<** or **>** to make each statement correct.

a 3·7 ● 3·9   **b** 5·83 ● 5·89   **c** 7·04 ● 7·40

d 8·364 g ● 8·299 g   **e** 6·9 cm ● 6·79 cm   **f** 0·074 ml ● 0·08 ml

2 Copy and write a number to make each statement correct.

a 7·5 < ■ < 8·2   **b** 6·9 > ■ > 6·1   **c** 8·03 < ■ < 8·05

d 5·7 < ■ < 5·8   **e** 4·1 > ■ > 4·0   **f** 6·13 < ■ < 6·14

3 These pupils took part in activities for charity.
List the results for each activity in order, starting with
the smallest.

Name	Amount lifted	Height jumped	Money collected
Jo	1·567 kg	1·17 m	£3·46
Dan	1885 g	98 cm	207p
Ed	1904 g	0·89 m	£2·70
Louise	1·639 kg	116 cm	94p
Lennox	1576 g	1·06 m	£0·96

Let's investigate

4 Sharon used these digits and zero to make 3 decimal numbers.

| 1 | 2 | 3 | 4 | 5 | 6 | 7 | 8 | 9 |

Each number was less than 1 and each had 3 decimal places.
She wrote them in order.

0·172   0·493   0·856

a What is the difference between Sharon's smallest and largest numbers?

b Investigate making 3 decimal numbers so that the difference between the smallest and largest numbers is as small as possible.

? What if the difference between the smallest and largest numbers was as large as possible?

Let's practise

1 Round to the nearest 10.

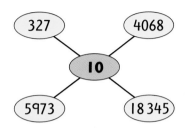

2 Round to the nearest 100.

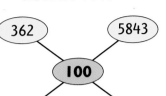

3 Round to the nearest 1000.

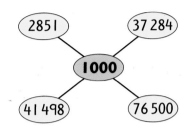

4 Write each mass of sugar to the nearest:

- 100 g
- 10 g.

a  **b** 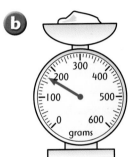 **c**

5

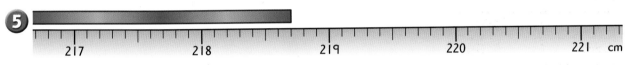

How long is the ribbon to the nearest:

a 100 centimetres **b** 10 centimetres **c** centimetre

d $\frac{1}{10}$ centimetre **e** $\frac{1}{100}$ metre **f** metre?

Let's play   A game for 2

- Player 1 writes a 5-digit number with 2 decimal places.
- Player 2 writes the number rounded to:
    - ◆ the nearest whole number
    - ◆ 1 decimal place.
- Player 2 scores 1 point for each correct answer (agreed with player 1).
- Players change roles.

The winner is the player with more points after 3 games each.

Let's practise

1 Write the temperatures (°C) in order, lowest first.

a 1, ⁻9, ⁻6, ⁻2, 3

b ⁻2·4, ⁻5, 4·2, ⁻8, 7

c ⁻17, 15, ⁻24, 13, ⁻11

d ⁻18·6, ⁻45°, 27, ⁻18·3, 0

2 ⁻4 is marked on this number line.

a Write 3 pairs of numbers that ⁻4 lies half way between.

b Write 3 pairs of numbers that ⁻6 lies half way between.

c Write 3 pairs of numbers that ⁻1 lies half way between.

Anders Celsius (1701–1744)

Invented the Celsius thermometer with 0° for the boiling point of water and 100° for its freezing point. After his death the scale was reversed to what we know as the centigrade scale.

Let's play   A game for 2

Take turns to:

- Choose 1 number from each bag below.
- Add them or find the difference between them.
- If the answer is in the grid, put a counter on it.

The winner is the first player to get 4 counters in a line, in any direction.

You need
counters in 2 colours

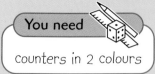

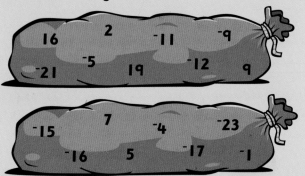

⁻15	7	⁻2	⁻26	28	⁻3
8	42	⁻16	⁻10	23	36
⁻26	⁻14	⁻12	1	⁻7	15
⁻16	⁻13	⁻29	2	⁻9	⁻35
⁻4	⁻10	9	⁻5	25	11
3	17	4	⁻1	⁻20	6

Let's practise

1 Copy and complete, calculating mentally.

a 14 + 29 = ☐   **b** ⁻53 + 72 = ☐   **c** ⁻63 + 37 = ☐   **d** ⁻42 + 53 = ☐

14 − ⁻29 = ☐   ⁻53 − ⁻72 = ☐   ⁻63 − ⁻37 = ☐   ⁻42 − ⁻53 = ☐

Use a calculator to check each answer.
Draw the keys that you pressed for **d**.

2 Copy and complete, calculating mentally.

a 17 + ⁻14 = ☐   **b** 42 + ⁻56 = ☐   **c** ⁻71 + ⁻49 = ☐   **d** ⁻65 + ⁻29 = ☐

17 − 14 = ☐   42 − 56 = ☐   ⁻71 − 49 = ☐   ⁻65 − 29 = ☐

Use a calculator to check each answer.
Draw the keys that you pressed for **d**.

Let's investigate

3 Copy and complete, using a calculator.

a $\dfrac{8.4 - 4.8}{8.4 + 4.8}$ **b** $\dfrac{8.4 + 4.8}{8.4 - 4.8}$

c $\dfrac{4.2 - 2.4}{4.2 + 2.4}$ **d** $\dfrac{4.2 + 2.4}{4.2 - 2.4}$

e $\dfrac{2.1 - 1.2}{2.1 + 1.2}$ **f** $\dfrac{2.1 + 1.2}{2.1 - 1.2}$

Explain any patterns you notice.

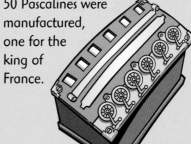

Blaise Pascal (1623–1662)

Pascal invented a calculator called the Pascaline in 1645, in order to help his father work on his accounts. About 50 Pascalines were manufactured, one for the king of France.

4 **a** Carry out the same calculations as in **3a** and **b** using the numbers 3·1 and 1·3.

b Find other calculations that have the same answers.

Let's practise

1 Find each product.

   a $2 \times 5 \times 7$ **b** $3 \times 7 \times 11$ **c** $2 \times 3 \times 5 \times 7$

   d $2^2 \times 3^2$ **e** $3^2 \times 5^2$ **f** $2^2 \times 3^2 \times 5^2$

2 Draw a factor tree for each of these numbers and complete the statements.

$18 = 2 \times 3^2$

   a   6

        $6 = \blacksquare \times \blacksquare$

   b   9

        $9 = 3^{\blacksquare}$

   c   30

        $30 = \blacksquare \times \blacksquare \times \blacksquare$

   d   36

        $36 = 2^{\blacksquare} \times 3^{\blacksquare}$

   e   ② ③ ⑤ ②

        $\blacksquare = 2^2 \times 3 \times 5$

Let's investigate

3 Kieran drew 2 different factor trees for the number 12.

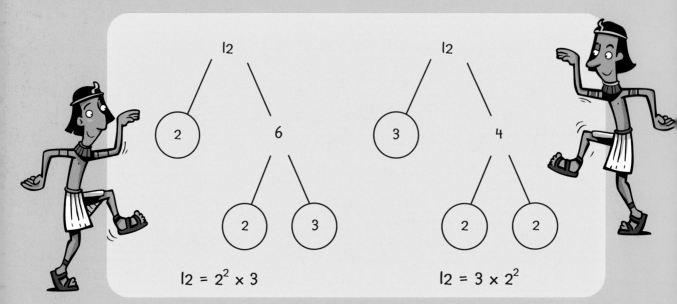

$12 = 2^2 \times 3$ $12 = 3 \times 2^2$

Investigate and compare different factor trees for multiples of 12 from 12 to 72.

Let's practise

① This is a test for divisibility by 7, without dividing.

   ⓐ Write the number.   1043

   ⓑ Delete the last digit.   104̶3̶

   ⓒ Double the deleted digit and place   104
       it under the last remaining digit.   <u> – 6</u>
                                         98

   ⓓ Subtract it from the remaining number.

   ⓔ Repeat **b** to **d** until a single-digit   9̶8̶
       positive or negative integer is reached. <u>– 16</u>
                                      ⁻7

   ⓕ If the single digit is ⁻7, 0 or 7 then the
       number is divisible by 7.

   ⓖ If the single digit is not ⁻7, 0 or 7 then
       the number is not divisible by 7

Use the test for the numbers 2933 and 5024.

Check by dividing the numbers by 7.

Pythagoras (c.570 – c.480 BCE)

Pythagoras was a Greek philosopher who made many important mathematical discoveries.

He is believed to have said: 'Number is the origin of all things, and the law of number is the key that unlocks the secrets of the universe.'

Let's investigate

② Daisy found all the divisors of 18, and then of 20.

18 is divisible by: 1 and 18   20 is divisible by: 1 and 20
                    2 and 9   2 and 10
                    3 and 6   4 and 5

Investigate the divisors of each integer from 40 to 50 and list them as pairs.

● Every number is divisible by 1 and itself.

● Try dividing the number by 2, then 3, then 4, and so on until the pairs start to
   repeat, e.g.   1 and 18
                    2 and 9
                    3 and 6
                    6 and 3

   This means you have found all the possible divisors.

? What if you investigated the divisors of a 3-digit number? Try some between 100 and 124. Remember to use tests of divisibility to help you find all the divisors.

Let's practise

1 Copy and complete.

a $2^2 + 3^2 = \blacksquare$ **b** $4^2 + 1^2 = \blacksquare$ **c** $6^2 + 5^2 = \blacksquare$

d $10^2 + 1^2 = \blacksquare$ **e** $5^2 + 3^2 = \blacksquare$ **f** $3^2 + 1^2 = \blacksquare$

g $8^2 + 2^2 = \blacksquare$ **h** $7^2 + 5^2 = \blacksquare$ **i** $9^2 + 11^2 = \blacksquare$

2 Copy and complete.

a $10^2 - 6^2 = \blacksquare$ **b** $3^2 - 1^2 = \blacksquare$ **c** $6^2 - 5^2 = \blacksquare$

d $4^2 - 2^2 = \blacksquare$ **e** $5^2 - 2^2 = \blacksquare$ **f** $7^2 - 2^2 = \blacksquare$

g $8^2 - 6^2 = \blacksquare$ **h** $2^2 - 1^2 = \blacksquare$ **i** $12^2 - 9^2 = \blacksquare$

3 Copy and complete.

a $7^2 - 5^2 = \blacksquare$
$(7 + 5) \times (7 - 5) = \blacksquare$

b $10^2 - 3^2 = \blacksquare$
$(10 + 3) \times (10 - 3) = \blacksquare$

c $15^2 - 11^2 = \blacksquare$
$(15 + 11) \times (15 - 11) = \blacksquare$

d $21^2 - 19^2 = \blacksquare$
$(21 + 19) \times (21 - 19) = \blacksquare$

Write what you notice about
each pair of answers.

Let's investigate

4 **a** Can you find a square number
that, when divided by 3, has a
remainder of 2?

b Can you predict what remainder
you will get when you divide
16^2 by 3?

Pascal (1623–1662)

Square numbers can be found in what is known as
Pascal's triangle.

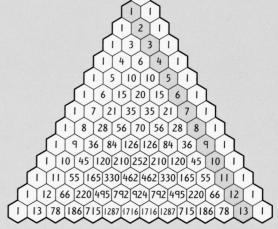

On the third diagonal, pairs of consecutive numbers
add to make square numbers.

What other patterns do you notice in the triangle?

Let's practise

1 Which of these products has the largest value?

$2^2 \times 2^2 \times 2^2 \times 2^2 \times 2^2 \times 2^2$

$3^2 \times 3^2 \times 3^2 \times 3^2 \times 3^2$

$4^2 \times 4^2 \times 4^2 \times 4^2$

$5^2 \times 5^2 \times 5^2$

$6^2 \times 6^2$

2
- Fold a piece of paper in half (1 fold). Open it and record the number of sections you have made. (2)
  You can also write this as $2 = 2^1$

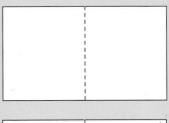

- Fold another piece of paper and then fold in half again (2 folds).
  Record the number of sections you have made. ($4 = 2^2$)

- Continue with new pieces of paper, folding and recording as many times as you can.

Let's investigate

3 Sally used her calculator to find:
$$1^2 = 1$$
$$11^2 = 121$$
$$111^2 = 12\,321$$
and noticed a pattern developing.

Investigate what pattern develops if Sally begins with 3^2, 33^2 and so on.

 What if you used the square of another single digit to begin a pattern?

Nicomachus of Gerasa (c.60 – c.120)

This Greek observed some of the properties of Pascal's triangle almost 1500 years before Pascal wrote about them himself. In his book *Introductio Arithmetica* (Introduction to Arithmetic), Nicomachus noticed that:
'every square number ... is made up of two successive triangular numbers.'

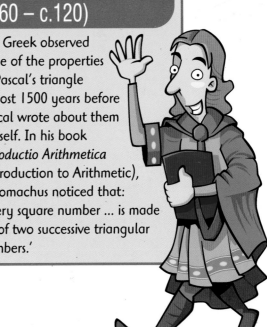

Let's practise

1 Copy and complete.

a $7^2 = \blacksquare$ **b** $12^2 = \blacksquare$ **c** $20^2 = \blacksquare$ **d** $25^2 = \blacksquare$ **e** $17^2 = \blacksquare$

Let's play A game for 2

You need

2 dice

Take turns.

- Player 1 secretly rolls 2 dice and uses the numbers to make a secret 2-digit number.
- Player 1 squares the number using a calculator and tells player 2 the answer.
- Player 2 guesses the original number and uses a calculator to check it.
- Player 1 counts the number of guesses before the original number is found.
- Play the game 5 times.

The winner is the player with the fewer guesses.

My number squared is 625.

I think your number is 23.

Let's investigate

2 Rashid thinks there is a pattern in the 'digital roots' of these products.

1 × 1 × 1 = 1	2 × 2 × 2 = 8	3 × 3 × 3 = 27
↓	↓	↓
1	8	9
4 × 4 × 4 = 64	5 × 5 × 5 = 125	6 × 6 × 6 = 216
↓	↓	↓
1	8	9

a What is the pattern that Rashid thinks he has found?

b Investigate for numbers up to 20 × 20 × 20 to check the pattern.

 What if you investigated patterns in the units digits of these products?

Let's practise

1 **(a)** $\sqrt{4} \times \sqrt{100} = \blacksquare$
$\sqrt{400} = \blacksquare$

(b) $\sqrt{9} \times \sqrt{100} = \blacksquare$
$\sqrt{900} = \blacksquare$

(c) $\sqrt{16} \times \sqrt{100} = \blacksquare$
$\sqrt{1600} = \blacksquare$

(d) $\sqrt{40\,000} = \blacksquare$

(e) $\sqrt{90\,000} = \blacksquare$

(f) $\sqrt{160\,000} = \blacksquare$

2 Copy and complete. A calculator may help you.

(a) $9 \longrightarrow$ [find its square] $\longrightarrow \blacksquare \longrightarrow$ [find its square root] $\longrightarrow \blacksquare$

(b) $38 \longrightarrow$ [find its square] $\longrightarrow \blacksquare \longrightarrow$ [find its square root] $\longrightarrow \blacksquare$

Write about what you notice. Explain why.

3 Copy and complete. A calculator may help you.

(a) $7 \longrightarrow$ [find its square root] $\longrightarrow \blacksquare \longrightarrow$ [find its square] $\longrightarrow \blacksquare$

(b) $31 \longrightarrow$ [find its square root] $\longrightarrow \blacksquare \longrightarrow$ [find its square] $\longrightarrow \blacksquare$

Write about what you notice. Explain why.

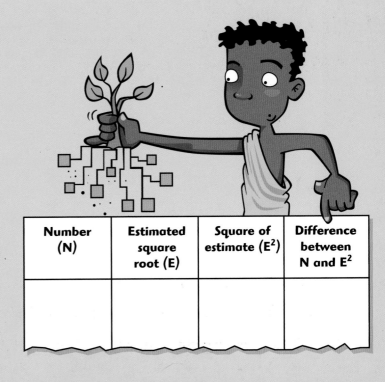

Lets play A game for 2

Take turns to:

- Choose a 2-digit number that is not a square number.

- Record this number in this table (N) and estimate the square root to the nearest tenth (E).

- Use the calculator to find the square of your estimate (E^2).

- Calculate the difference between N and E^2.

The winner is the player with the smallest total of differences after 3 rounds.

Number (N)	Estimated square root (E)	Square of estimate (E^2)	Difference between N and E^2

Let's practise

1 Copy and complete. Use **<** or **>**.

a $\frac{1}{2}$ ◯ $\frac{7}{10}$ **b** $\frac{3}{8}$ ◯ $\frac{1}{2}$ **c** $\frac{1}{2}$ ◯ $\frac{2}{3}$ **d** $\frac{7}{15}$ ◯ $\frac{1}{2}$

e $\frac{1}{4}$ ◯ $\frac{2}{9}$ **f** $\frac{2}{3}$ ◯ $\frac{5}{8}$ **g** $\frac{5}{7}$ ◯ $\frac{3}{4}$ **h** $\frac{1}{3}$ ◯ $\frac{2}{7}$

i $\frac{3}{8}$ ◯ $\frac{2}{5}$ **j** $\frac{4}{7}$ ◯ $\frac{3}{5}$ **k** $\frac{5}{6}$ ◯ $\frac{4}{9}$ **l** $\frac{5}{12}$ ◯ $\frac{4}{7}$

2 Write these fractions and mixed numbers in order, smallest first.

a $\frac{3}{4}$, $\frac{2}{3}$ and $\frac{5}{6}$ **b** $1\frac{3}{10}$, $1\frac{1}{5}$ and $1\frac{3}{4}$

c $2\frac{1}{10}$, $2\frac{1}{2}$ and $2\frac{2}{5}$ **d** $\frac{7}{9}$, $1\frac{2}{3}$, $\frac{3}{4}$, $2\frac{1}{5}$ and $2\frac{2}{7}$

3 Write 3 fractions that lie between each pair of fractions.

a $\frac{1}{4}$ and $\frac{1}{2}$ **b** $\frac{1}{2}$ and $\frac{1}{3}$ **c** $\frac{1}{4}$ and $\frac{1}{5}$

d $\frac{1}{3}$ and $\frac{2}{3}$ **e** $\frac{3}{5}$ and $\frac{4}{5}$ **f** $\frac{5}{6}$ and $\frac{11}{12}$

Let's investigate 🖩

4 Lauren chooses the fraction $\frac{2}{3}$.

She inverts it (turns it upside down) to get $\frac{3}{2}$.

She finds that $\frac{2}{3}$ is nearer to 1 than $\frac{3}{2}$ is because

$1 - \frac{2}{3} = \frac{1}{3} = 0 \cdot 333$ to 3 decimal places and $\frac{3}{2} - 1 = \frac{1}{2} = 0 \cdot 5$.

Investigate fractions and their inverses to find which is nearer to 1.

Use a calculator to help.

Write about your conclusions and explain your reasoning.

> ## Fractions
>
> Ahmes, an Egyptian scribe, wrote a series of mathematical problems on papyrus in 1650 BCE, now known as the Rhind Papyrus. One of the problems involved the use of fractions.

Let's practise

1 Copy and complete.

a $\frac{48}{9} = 5\frac{1}{\square}$ **b** $\frac{93}{6} = 15\frac{1}{\square}$ **c** $\frac{22}{8} = 2\frac{3}{\square}$

d $\frac{34}{4} = 8\frac{\square}{2}$ **e** $\frac{68}{10} = 6\frac{\square}{5}$ **f** $\frac{102}{14} = 7\frac{\square}{7}$

2 Copy and complete.

a $4\frac{6}{9} = \frac{\square}{3}$ **b** $7\frac{2}{4} = \frac{\square}{2}$ **c** $3\frac{8}{12} = \frac{\square}{3}$

d $6\frac{15}{20} = \frac{27}{\square}$ **e** $9\frac{4}{6} = \frac{29}{\square}$ **f** $8\frac{4}{10} = \frac{42}{\square}$

3 Write the fractions that match the statements.

a Half the size of one sixth.

b Three times as much as two sevenths.

c One quarter of the size of eight hundredths.

d Half the size of one eleventh.

e Twice as much as one fifth.

f Three times as much as three eighteenths.

g Twice the size of one thirteenth.

Egyptian fractions

Egyptians only used unit fractions, that is, fractions with 1 as the numerator, such as $\frac{1}{2}$ or $\frac{1}{4}$. To make bigger fractions they had to add these unit fractions together. The only exceptions were $\frac{2}{3}$ and $\frac{3}{4}$, which had their own symbols.

Let's solve problems

4 a Use interlocking cubes to make the smallest possible cuboid that has:

- one half of one quarter of its cubes red
- three times as much as one eighth of its cubes blue
- one third of one half of its cubes green
- twice one sixth of its cubes yellow.

b How many cubes are there in the cuboid?

c How many cubes of each colour are in the cuboid?

d What is the next largest cuboid that satisfies the same 4 conditions?

You need

interlocking cubes

Let's practise

1 What fraction of:

a 1 metre is 65 centimetres

b 1 litre is 25 millilitres

c 1 hour is 27 minutes

d 6 kilometres is 500 metres?

2 What fraction of a turn is: **a** 30°   **b** 45°   **c** 300°?

> **You need**
>
> 6 cards, red and blue counters
>
> $\frac{1}{3}$ $\frac{1}{4}$ $\frac{1}{6}$ $\frac{1}{9}$ $\frac{1}{12}$ $\frac{1}{18}$

Let's play A game for 2

● Choose which colour counters each of you will use.

● Shuffle the cards and place them face down in a pile.

● Take turns to turn over the top card of the pile.
  Cover this fraction of the grid below with your counters.

● Continue until all the cards have been turned over.

The winner is the player with more squares covered.

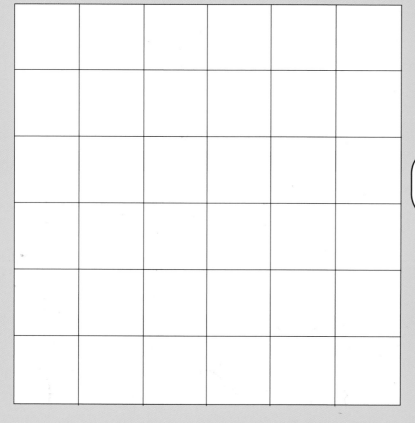

> I have $\frac{1}{4}$.
> I will cover 9 small squares.

Design a game of your own with a larger grid and different fraction cards.

et's practise

1 **a** Use fractions from the box to make 4 sets of 3 equivalent fractions.

$\frac{1}{8}$	$\frac{27}{36}$	$\frac{4}{10}$	$\frac{1}{3}$	$\frac{3}{9}$	$\frac{2}{16}$
$\frac{3}{24}$	$\frac{8}{20}$	$\frac{2}{5}$	$\frac{9}{12}$	$\frac{2}{6}$	$\frac{3}{4}$

b Add 3 more equivalent fractions to each set.

c Write about the relationship between numerators and denominators in each set.

2 Write 2 equivalent fractions to describe the fraction of each shape that is:
• blue • red.

a

b

c

d

e

f

3 Write the highest common factor of each pair of numbers.

a 40 and 50   **b** 12 and 16   **c** 18 and 63

d 12 and 20   **e** 42 and 56   **f** 24 and 30

g 45 and 54   **h** 12 and 96   **i** 36 and 45

4 Copy and cancel each fraction to its simplest equivalent form.
(The answers to question 3 will help you.)

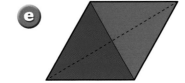

a $\frac{40}{50}$ **b** $\frac{12}{16}$ **c** $\frac{18}{63}$ **d** $\frac{12}{20}$

e $\frac{42}{56}$ **f** $\frac{24}{30}$ **g** $\frac{45}{54}$ **h** $\frac{12}{96}$

et's investigate

5 Simon writes the equivalent fraction statement: $\frac{13}{26} = \frac{31}{62}$

He notices that the digits in the numerators and in the denominators are reversed.

Investigate other pairs of equivalent fractions like this.

Look for and write about the relationship between the digits in each fraction.

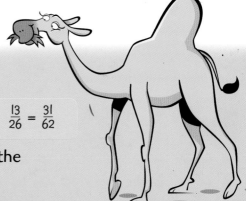

Let's practise

1 Find:

a $\frac{1}{8} + \frac{1}{8}$ **b** $\frac{1}{8} + \frac{1}{8} + \frac{1}{8}$ **c** $\frac{1}{4} + \frac{1}{8}$

d $\frac{1}{4} + \frac{1}{8} + \frac{1}{8}$ **e** $\frac{1}{4} + \frac{1}{4} + \frac{1}{8}$ **f** $\frac{1}{2} + \frac{1}{8}$

g $\frac{1}{2} + \frac{1}{8} + \frac{1}{8}$ **h** $\frac{1}{2} + \frac{1}{4}$ **i** $\frac{1}{2} + \frac{1}{4} + \frac{1}{8}$.

2 Find:

a $1 - \frac{1}{8}$ **b** $1 - \frac{1}{8} - \frac{1}{8}$ **c** $1 - \frac{1}{4}$

d $1 - \frac{1}{4} - \frac{1}{8}$ **e** $1 - \frac{1}{4} - \frac{1}{8} - \frac{1}{8}$ **f** $1 - \frac{1}{4} - \frac{1}{4}$

g $1 - \frac{1}{2}$ **h** $1 - \frac{1}{2} - \frac{1}{8}$ **i** $1 - \frac{1}{2} - \frac{1}{8} - \frac{1}{8}$.

3 Find:

a $\frac{1}{2} + \frac{1}{4}$ **b** $\frac{1}{2} + \frac{1}{4} + \frac{1}{8}$ **c** $\frac{1}{2} + \frac{1}{4} + \frac{1}{8} + \frac{1}{16}$

d $\frac{1}{2} + \frac{1}{4} + \frac{1}{8} + \frac{1}{16} + \frac{1}{32}$ **e** $\frac{1}{2} + \frac{1}{4} + \frac{1}{8} + \frac{1}{16} + \frac{1}{32} + \frac{1}{64}$.

Let's investigate

4 Abigail makes 4 different fractions, each with 3 as the denominator:

$$\frac{4}{3} \quad \frac{6}{3} \quad \frac{2}{3} \quad \frac{7}{3}$$

Euclid (c.330 – c.275 BCE)

This Greek mathematician studied in the famous academy in Athens.

He devised a method for finding the highest common factor of two numbers, known today as Euclid's Algorithm.

She tries to use all the fractions to make 1 by adding or subtracting:

$$\frac{7}{3} - \frac{6}{3} + \frac{4}{3} - \frac{2}{3} =$$

a Copy and complete her calculation.

b Investigate making 1 by adding or subtracting 4 different fractions, all with a denominator of 3.

? What if the 4 fractions had a denominator of 4, 5, 6... ?

Let's practise

1 What fraction of each shape is red?

a 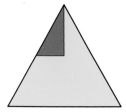 **b**  **c**

2 What fraction of the larger shape is the smaller one?

a   **b**   **c**   **d**

3 What fraction of:

a I metre is 55 centimetres

b I hour is 40 minutes

c I kilogram is 24 grams

d I yard is I foot

e I metre is 80 centimetres

f I hour is 33 minutes

g I kilogram is 101 grams

h I foot is 9 inches?

Write each fraction in its lowest terms.

Let's solve problems

4 Rob and Bella are studying a map to find their way home.

a They start at 12:00 and use a watch to help them turn through 90°. What fraction of a turn have they taken?

b They are now facing east. They walk for $\frac{3}{10}$ of I hour. What time do they stop for their next instruction?

c They are still facing east and make a $\frac{3}{8}$ clockwise turn. What direction are they facing now?

d The time is now 12:35. They stop walking at 12:55. For what fraction of an hour did they walk this time?

e They reach their destination. They finally turn clockwise through 135°. What direction are they facing at the end?

Let's practise

1 Copy and complete.

$\frac{3}{8}$ of 48 has the same value as (48 ÷ 8) × 3 = 18

a $\frac{2}{3}$ of 15 has the same value as (▢ ÷ ▢) × ▢ = ▢

b $\frac{4}{7}$ of 21 has the same value as (▢ ÷ ▢) × ▢ = ▢

c $\frac{7}{9}$ of 45 has the same value as (▢ ÷ ▢) × ▢ = ▢

d $\frac{3}{5}$ of 35 has the same value as (▢ ÷ ▢) × ▢ = ▢

2 Find:

a one fifth of 40 m

b two thirds of 150 g

c $\frac{1}{3}$ of 24 cm

d $\frac{3}{8}$ of 160 ml

e $\frac{9}{10}$ of 1 metre

f $\frac{3}{4}$ of 56 g

g $\frac{2}{7}$ of 42 litres

h four ninths of 63 cm

i $\frac{5}{6}$ of 72 kg

j seven tenths of 20 metres.

3 Find:

a $\frac{1}{2}$ of ($\frac{1}{2}$ of ($\frac{1}{2}$ of ($\frac{1}{2}$ of £64)))

b $\frac{2}{3}$ of ($\frac{2}{3}$ of ($\frac{2}{3}$ of ($\frac{2}{3}$ of 81 km)))

c $\frac{3}{4}$ of ($\frac{3}{4}$ of ($\frac{3}{4}$ of ($\frac{3}{4}$ of 256 kg)))

d $\frac{1}{10}$ of ($\frac{1}{10}$ of ($\frac{1}{10}$ of ($\frac{1}{10}$ of 10 000 l))).

Let's investigate

You need

set of 0–9 cards

4 Investigate using 4 different digits from 0 to 9 to complete the sentence:

$\frac{▢}{▢}$ of ▢▢ = 6.

? What if the sentence was $\frac{▢}{▢}$ of ▢▢ = 7?

Let's solve problems

1 The table shows the nutritional content of a jar of drinking chocolate.

a What percentage of a 28 g serving is:

- protein
- carbohydrate
- fat
- fibre
- sodium?

Write your answers to 1 decimal place.

Per 28 g serving	
protein	2·2 g
carbohydrate (of which sugar is	18·7 g 16·4 g)
fat (of which saturates	3·8 g 3·4 g)
fibre	0·6 g
sodium	0·2 g

b What percentage of the carbohydrate is sugar?

c What percentage of the fat is non-saturates?

2 A yellow square is placed on top of a green square.

What percentage of the green square is covered by the yellow square?

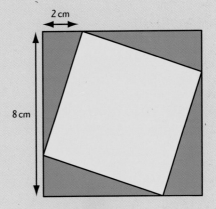

2 cm

8 cm

3 The chart shows what children in Year 6 do at lunchtime. 18 children have a school dinner.

a How many children are in Year 6?

b How many more have a packed lunch than go home?

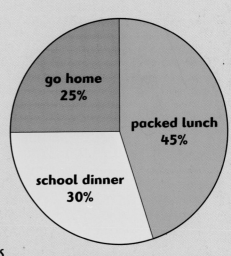

go home 25%

packed lunch 45%

school dinner 30%

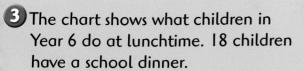 What if the percentages were:

- 24% school dinner
- 20% go home
- 56% packed lunch?

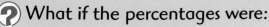

Work out the answers to the same questions as in **3** without a calculator.

Let's practise

1 Find: **a** 10% of £357 **b** 11% of £540 **c** 9% of £683.

Let's solve problems

2 The table shows the changes in price of flats and houses last year in Scarby.

What were the prices of each type of property at the end of June and at the end of December?

Type of accommodation	Price on 1 January	Percentage change Jan.-end June	Percentage change July–end Dec.
Flat	£26 000	+ 10%	+ 15%
Terraced house	£48 000	+ 5%	+ 4%
Three-bedroomed house	£92 000	+ 8%	− 5%
Detached house	£142 000	+ 6%	− 20%

3 In a January sale the price of a £12 shirt was reduced by 10%.
In February the sale price was increased by 10%.

a What was the price of the shirt in the January sale?

b What was the price of the shirt in February?

c Explain why the pre-sale and post-sale prices are different.

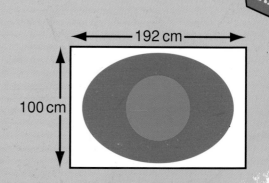

4 30% of this rectangle is red, 20% is green and the rest is white.

a What area of the rectangle is red?

b What area of the rectangle is green?

c What area of the rectangle is white?

192 cm

100 cm

Let's practise

1 Use $\frac{1}{5} = 0.2$ and multiplication to convert each fraction to a decimal.

$\frac{3}{5} = 0.2 \times 3 = 0.6$

a $\frac{4}{5}$ **b** $\frac{6}{5}$ **c** $\frac{8}{5}$ **d** $\frac{12}{5}$

2 Use $\frac{1}{4} = 0.25$ and multiplication to convert each fraction to a decimal.

$\frac{3}{4} = 0.25 \times 3 = 0.75$

a $\frac{5}{4}$ **b** $\frac{7}{4}$ **c** $\frac{9}{4}$ **d** $\frac{11}{4}$

To change pints to litres you can get a rough answer by multiplying the number of pints by $\frac{3}{5}$.

Pints, quarts, pottles and gallons

Look at extract from the *Gauger and Measurer's Companion* (1694). There are many old units of measurement. Can you find some more?

Of Liquid Measure

	Pints	Qu.	Pot.
In one Gallon are	8	4	2
One Pottle	4	2	1
In one Quart	2	1	0

3 Use Matt's method to convert these measurements to litres.

a 20 pints   **b** 35 pints   **c** 45 pints   **d** 25 pints

e 55 pints   **f** 15 pints   **g** 50 pints   **h** 30 pints

Let's play   A game for 2

Take turns to:

- Choose 1 percentage card and 1 number from the rectangle.
- Find the percentage of the number and record it.

15% of 300 = 45

Check your answer using a calculator.

- If the answer is in the pyramid, score 1 point.

The winner is the first to score 5 points.

75%	5%

15%	60%

300	50	12	360
900	140	120	112

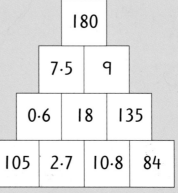

Pyramid:

	180	
	7.5	9
0.6	18	135
105	2.7	10.8	84

Let's practise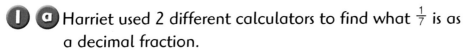

1 **a** Harriet used 2 different calculators to find what $\frac{1}{7}$ is as a decimal fraction.

This is what she saw on the displays:

0.1428571	0.142857142

Which answer is correct?

Explain why the answers are different.

b Without using a calculator, write $\frac{1}{7}$ as a decimal fraction to 12 decimal places. Explain any patterns in the digits of the decimal fraction.

2 Use your calculators to find the unit fractions $\frac{1}{2}$, $\frac{1}{3}$, $\frac{1}{4}$, ... , $\frac{1}{20}$ as decimal fractions.

Write about what you find out.

> **You need**
>
> 2 calculators that display a different number of digits

John Napier (1550–1617)

Napier was the first mathematician to always use the decimal point to separate the whole-number part from the fractional part of a number. This usage became standard in Great Britain, although many other European countries continued to use a decimal comma instead.

Let's investigate

3 **a** Harriet found that $\frac{1}{7}$ = 0·142 857 142 857 142 8...
What do the 3 dots at the end of the digits mean?

b We can write $\frac{1}{7}$ as 0·$\dot{1}$42 85$\dot{7}$ because the digits 142 857 recur (repeat). Explain what the 2 dots mean.

c Investigate the recurring decimal fractions for $\frac{2}{7}$, $\frac{3}{7}$, $\frac{4}{7}$, $\frac{5}{7}$ and $\frac{6}{7}$.

? What if the fractions were $\frac{1}{13}$, $\frac{2}{13}$, $\frac{3}{13}$, ..., $\frac{12}{13}$?

Let's practise

1 Estimate the proportion of each flag that is:

● red   ● blue.

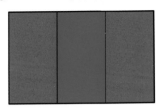

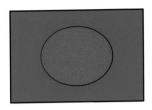

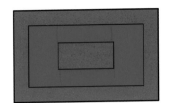

2 The charts show what colours children in Years 4, 5 and 6 liked best.
Estimate the proportion of children in each year that chose each colour.

a others

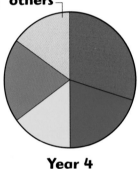

Year 4

b others

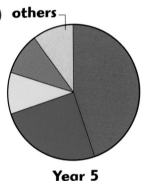

Year 5

c others

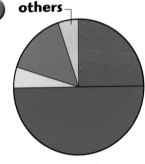

Year 6

Let's solve problems

3 In a packet of 100 sweets, 25 are red and 75 are other colours.

a What proportion is red?   **b** What proportion is not red?

Write each answer as a fraction, decimal and percentage.

4 In a tank of 30 fish, 27 are gold and the rest are black.

a What proportion is gold?   **b** What proportion is black?

Write each answer as a fraction, decimal and percentage.

5 Eleanor and Arash are sorting counters.
The table lists how many they have of each colour.

	Number of counters				
	red	**blue**	**yellow**	**orange**	**green**
Eleanor	80	110	75	100	35
Arash	120	130	80	125	45

What proportion of each colour do Eleanor and Arash each have?

Don't forget to explain how you solved each problem.

Let's practise

1 Copy each ratio and write it in its simplest form.

a 4 : 12   **b** 12 : 18   **c** 2 : 22   **d** 10 : 15   **e** 8 : 32

f 21 : 14   **g** 10 : 35   **h** 24 : 30   **i** 80 : 104   **j** 63 : 108

2 Estimate the ratio of yellow to green in each flag.

a 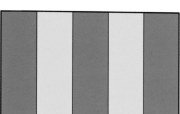   **b** 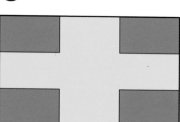   **c**

Let's solve problems

3 The table shows the number of home and away supporters at 4 Manford United games.

Supporters	Game 1	Game 2	Game 3	Game 4
Manford United	36 000	28 000	32 500	30 000
Visitors	6000	4000	2500	1500

a What was the ratio of Manford United supporters to visitors at each game?

b At which game was the proportion of visiting supporters the greatest?

4 Sam and Ali divide £150 in the ratio 1 : 2.
Sam gets 1 part and Ali gets 2 parts. How much money do they each get?

5 240 kg of sand is divided into piles in the ratio 3 : 5.
How much sand will be in each pile?

6 Sue spent her savings of £40 on books and clothes in the ratio 1 : 3.
How much did she spend on clothes?

Let's practise

1 Make up a word problem for each number statement.

a $(17 + 87) \times 10 = 1040$ **b** $76 - (54 \div 2) = 49$

c $(42 + 39) \times 3 = 243$ **d** $18 + 15 + 23 - 34 = 22$

Let's solve problems

2 **a**

b

c

Hat and scarf cost £6·95
Hat, hat and scarf cost £10·95
What does a hat cost?
What does a scarf cost?

Can of drink and choc bar cost £1·10
Can, choc bar and choc bar cost £1.55
What does a choc bar cost?
What does a can cost?

Bag and belt cost £18·20
Bag, belt and belt and belt cost £25·80
What does a belt cost?
What does a bag cost?

3 In the room there are some people and some snakes.
There are 20 eyes and 12 legs.

How many people are there?
How many snakes are there?

4 In the swimming pool there are some people and some dolphins.
There are 22 eyes and 16 legs.

How many people are there?
How many dolphins are there?

5 In the pond there are some frogs and some fish.
There are 36 eyes and 36 legs.

How many frogs are there?
How many fish are there?

6 **a** About how long do you spend sitting down in school each day?

b How long is that in:
   ● I week   ● I term   ● I year?

c If you leave school at the end of Year 13, about how long will you have spent sitting down in school altogether?

> Remember that year R (reception) is the first year of school.

Let's practise

1 Copy and complete.

a $8 + 4 \times (2 + 6) + 3 = \square$

b $7 - 8 \div 2 = \square$

c $(3 + 2) \times 5 = \square$

d $6 \times (4 + 3) - 6 \times 2 = \square$

e $20 - \dfrac{(6 + 4)}{5} = \square$

f $\dfrac{(5 + 5 + 7)}{2} = \square$

Let's solve problems

2 A, B and C stand for different single-digit numbers. Find the values of A, B and C that match all 4 statements.

$A + B + C = 21$	$A \times C = 36$
$\dfrac{B}{2} = C$	$A + B - C = 13$

3 **a** P, Q, R and S stand for different single-digit numbers. Find the values of P, Q, R and S that match all 4 statements.

$P + Q + R + S = 20$	$Q \times 4 = P \times 3$
$P \times S - Q = R \times 3$	$\dfrac{(R + Q)}{(P + S)} = 1$

Enigma

The Enigma coding machine was used by the Nazis during World War II to send secret information.

The odds against anyone who did not know the settings being able to break its code were an amazing 150 million to one.

b Make up some similar codes for a partner to solve.

Let's investigate

4 Natasha used the 4 digits, 3 of the operations and both pairs of brackets to make a whole number.

$(8 - 3) \times (6 + 4) = 50$

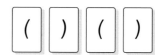

Investigate making different whole numbers.

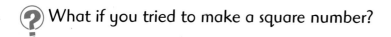

? What if you tried to make a square number?

Let's practise

To change miles to kilometres you can get a rough answer by first dividing by 5, then multiplying by 8.

Use Megan's tip to convert each measurement to kilometres.

a 20 miles   **b** 35 miles   **c** 45 miles   **d** 25 miles

e 55 miles   **f** 15 miles   **g** 50 miles   **h** 30 miles

2 Use the inverse operation to convert each measurement to miles.

Divide by 8 and multiply by 5.

a 24 km   **b** 40 km   **c** 56 km   **d** 72 km

e 88 km   **f** 32 km   **g** 48 km   **h** 64 km

3

To change kilograms to pounds (lbs) you can get a rough answer by first increasing the number of kilograms by one tenth, then multiplying by 2.

Use Sam's tip to convert each measurement to pounds.

a 20 kg   **b** 60 kg   **c** 150 kg   **d** 180 kg

e 210 kg   **f** 250 kg   **g** 320 kg   **h** 410 kg

Let's investigate

4 Start with a 2-digit number. Square each digit and add the answers. Keep doing this until the answer is a single digit.

$$89 \rightarrow \boxed{\begin{array}{l} 8^2 = 64 \\ 9^2 = 81 \end{array}} \rightarrow 145 \rightarrow \boxed{\begin{array}{l} 1^2 = 1 \\ 4^2 = 16 \\ 5^2 = 25 \end{array}} \rightarrow 42 \rightarrow \boxed{\begin{array}{l} 4^2 = 16 \\ 2^2 = 4 \end{array}} \rightarrow 20 \rightarrow \boxed{\begin{array}{l} 2^2 = 4 \\ 0^2 = 0 \end{array}} \rightarrow 4$$

Investigate doing this for different 2-digit numbers.

? What if you started with 3-digit numbers?

Let's practise

1
- **a** $\frac{1}{2}$ of 4·6
- **b** twice 3·7
- **c** half of 0·94
- **d** double 0·56
- **e** divide 0·78 by 2
- **f** $2 \times 4·9$
- **g** $\sqrt{81}$
- **h** 800^2

Let's solve problems

2

a Dan is twice as old as Dev. Dan is 56. How old is Dev?	**b** Sam is half as old as Alice. Alice is 96. How old is Sam?
c Twice as many people went to the pop concert on Saturday as on Sunday. 7900 went on Sunday. How many went on Saturday?	**d** Twice as many people went to the rock concert on Saturday as on Sunday. 13 200 went on Saturday. How many went on Sunday?
e Carol has twice as many CDs as Debbie. Carol has 94. How many has Debbie?	**f** Jo is half as old as Deepa. Jo is 38. How old is Deepa?
g There is double the number of tins of soup as tins of beans in a shop. There are 1340 tins of soup. How many tins of beans are there?	**h** Half as many children were in school today as yesterday. There were 790 children today. How many were there yesterday?
i Twice as many trains ran on Monday as on Sunday. There were 15 600 trains on Monday. How many ran on Sunday?	**j** Half as many people came to a football match this week as last week. Last week there were 17 400 people. How many were there this week?

Let's investigate

3 Investigate choosing 5 different numbers so that the sum of 3 of the numbers is double the sum of 2 of the numbers.

$\square + \square + \square = A$ $\square + \square = B$ A is double B

? What if the sum of the 3 numbers was half the sum of the 2 numbers?

Let's practise

1.
a) 97 − 76 = ▢
b) Add 48 to 62.
c) ▢ + 63 = 87
d) ▢ − 57 = 42
e) Decrease 52 by 37.
f) Increase 31 by 76.
g) 51 + ▢ = 89
h) 87 − ▢ = 42

Calculating with beads

An abacus uses beads to perform addition, subtraction, multiplication and division. Its earliest known use was in China c.500 BCE, although counting beads are thought to have been used in China more than 3000 years ago.

2. The sum of 2 numbers from the circles is equal to the number in the square.
The difference between 2 numbers from the circles is equal to the number in the square.
Write an addition and a subtraction sentence for each of these.

a)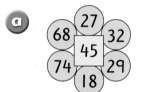

b)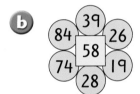

c)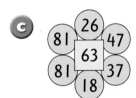

d)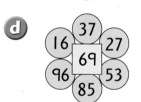

e)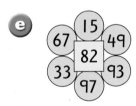

f)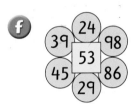

Let's investigate

3.
- Roll the dice.
- Use the key to find what each rolled number represents.
- Find the total of the 2 numbers.

You need
2 dice

Key			
1 ⟶ 64	4 ⟶ 67
2 ⟶ 65	5 ⟶ 68
3 ⟶ 66	6 ⟶ 69

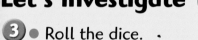

64 + 67 = 131

Predict what the most and least common totals will be.
Explain how you decided.

Investigate different totals by repeating the steps 19 more times.

- What is your most common total? Explain why.
- What is your least common total(s)? Explain why.
- Use a calculator to find the mean of the 20 totals.

Let's solve problems

1 Look at the pattern of numbers in these grids.
Work out the missing numbers A and B.

You need

a counter

1	4
8	3

6	1
9	2

4	3
9	A

2	B
26	15

2
- Choose a target number between 5 and 20.
- Move your counter through the maze from start to finish. Keep a running total.
- How many moves does it take you to finish on your target number?
- Choose another target number and try again.

Start on 20 → 8 → 7 → 9
6 → 9 → 6 → 11
4 → 7 → 13 → 10
11 → 8 → 11 → END

3 Copy the arrow diagram.

    a Arrange the multiples of 10 from 10 to 80 so that the sum of the numbers along each line is the same.

    b Find a different way to do it.

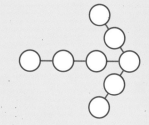

Let's investigate

4 Erin used all 9 digits in order, and added and subtracted them to make 11.

$$1 - 2 + 3 + 4 + 5 - 6 + 7 + 8 - 9 = 11$$

Investigate making numbers 1 to 30 using all 9 digits in order, but adding and subtracting them in a different way.

? What if the digits were in reverse order?

Let's practise

① Find the total of the 4 numbers in each grid.

ⓐ
15 342	165
23	68 912

ⓑ
305	29 463
3009	46 527

ⓒ
27 401	98 903
630	33 034

Let's play   A game for 2

You need

2 sets of 0–9 digit cards

- Each player chooses 5 different digits to make a 5-digit number.
- Each player then adds **53 827** to their number.
- A point is scored for each **4** in the answer.
- Repeat, using a different 5-digit number.

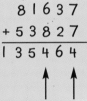

Scores 2 points

```
  8 1 6 3 7
+ 5 3 8 2 7
-----------
1 3 5 4 6 4
        ↑   ↑
```

The winner is the first player to score 10 points.

Let's solve problems

② Find the total in each headline.

ⓐ **Expected attendance of 83 407 exceeded by 5005**

ⓑ Vandals, who caused £459 120 damage so far this year, cause another £200 781

ⓒ A company manager who earns £452 972 a year received £20 935 in bonuses yesterday

ⓓ Last month's unemployment figure of 32 581 rises by 62 340

ⓔ Maths 'r' us bookshop reports takings up £30 591 from £48 901 at start of year

ⓕ **The £2 484 517 in unclaimed lottery winnings increased by £651 803 this week**

Let's practise

1 Find the triangle with the smallest total.

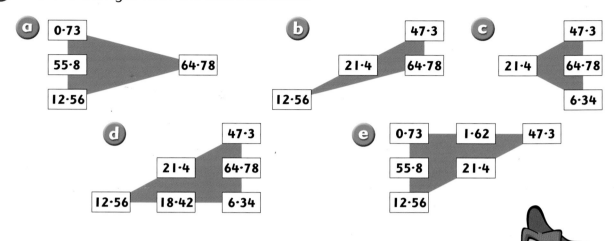

a) 0·73, 55·8, 64·78, 12·56

b) 47·3, 21·4, 64·78, 12·56

c) 47·3, 21·4, 64·78, 6·34

d) 47·3, 21·4, 64·78, 12·56, 18·42, 6·34

e) 0·73, 1·62, 47·3, 55·8, 21·4, 12·56

Let's solve problems

2 Find the missing numbers *a* to *d*.

X	Y	Z	X + Y + Z
8·75	47·34	17·76	*a*
6·87	39·43	*b*	68·13
7·63	*c*	42·92	53·44
d	8·46	21·55	38·33

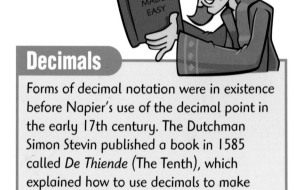

Decimals

Forms of decimal notation were in existence before Napier's use of the decimal point in the early 17th century. The Dutchman Simon Stevin published a book in 1585 called *De Thiende* (The Tenth), which explained how to use decimals to make calculations easier.

Let's investigate

3 Copy and complete the pattern. Find the answers.

11·1 + 1·11 =

22·2 + 2·22 =

33·3 + 3·33 =

44·4 + 4·44 =

- Look for a pattern in your answers.
- What do you notice about the hundredths and tenths digits in each answer?
- Find the differences between consecutive answers. What do you notice?

? What if the pattern began 111·1 + 1·111, 222·2 + 2·222, ...?

Let's practise

1 Subtract **41 976** from each number.

a 54 321   **b** 76 543   **c** 98 765

Write about patterns in the answers.

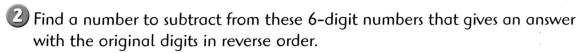

2 Find a number to subtract from these 6-digit numbers that gives an answer with the original digits in reverse order.

654 321   **765 432**   **987 654**

3 Find a number to subtract from these 7-digit numbers that gives an answer with the original digits in reverse order.

7 654 321   **8 765 432**   **9 876 543**

4 Find a number to subtract from these 8-digit numbers that gives an answer with the original digits in reverse order.

87 654 321   **98 765 432**

Let's solve problems

5 The digits 0 to 9 have been arranged to make a 5-digit number subtracted from a 5-digit number.

a Write about the pattern of digits in this group of subtractions.

98 765	−	43 210
87 654	−	32 109
76 543	−	21 098
65 432	−	10 987
54 321	−	09 876

Writing digits

The 10 digits we use today evolved from early forms of Indian numerals that were used in the Arabian empire and later in Europe.

Numerals used c.969

۱	۲	۳	۴	۶	۶	٧	۸	۹	۰
1	2	3	4	5	6	7	8	9	0

Numerals used c.1200

۱	2	3	۴	Y	6	۸	8	9
1	2	3	4	5	6	7	8	9

b Copy and complete each subtraction.

c Find the differences between consecutive answers.

d Write about any patterns you see.

Let's solve problems

1 **a** Copy and complete the magic square.
The total for each row, column or diagonal is 26·76.

9·39		6·11
5·64		
		8·45

b Draw another magic square by subtracting 1·78 from each number.
What is the total for each row, column or diagonal now?

Let's investigate

2 Cameron used the digits | 5 | 6 | 7 | 8 | 9 | to complete
this subtraction.

9·5 – 7·68 = 1·82

Investigate using the same 5 digits to complete the subtraction

 □·□ – □·□□   for answers between 0 and 1.

3 Copy and continue the pattern. Find the answers.

11·1 – 1·11 =
22·2 – 2·22 =
33·3 – 3·33 =
44·4 – 4·44 =

- Look for a pattern in your answers.
- What do you notice about the hundredths digit in each answer?
- What do you notice about the tenths digit in each answer?

? What if you found the difference between consecutive answers in the pattern?

Let's practise

1 Copy these questions.

Place a decimal point in each number so that the answers are between 0 and 20.

a 1 6 8 + 5 5 = ☐   **b** 3 3 1 − 1 1 7 = ☐   **c** 6 5 + 1 2 0 = ☐

d 2 7 + 6 3 1 = ☐   **e** 2 4 6 − 5 6 = ☐   **f** 2 0 9 − 1 1 0 = ☐

Let's solve problems

2 The row and column of this cross each add up to 1·3.
Arrange the decimal numbers

0·1   0·2   0·3   0·4   0·5   0·6

in a cross so that its row and column each add to:

a 1·1   **b** 1·2.

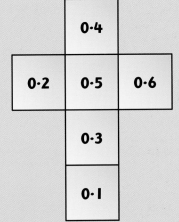

3 Here are 3 decimal number cards.

| 0·8 | | 0·6 | | 0·5 |

Each card has a different number with 1 decimal place on its other side.

The cards are thrown into the air. The 3 numbers that are visible when they land can have a total of: 1, 1·2, 1·3, 1·5, 1·6, 1·8, 1·9, or 2·1.

What is the number on the other side of each card?

Let's investigate

4 Rhys used the digits 9 to 1, in order, to make a calculation of 3 numbers each with 1 decimal place.

98·7 − 65·4 + 32·1 = 65·4

Investigate using the digits 9 to 1, in order, to make calculations of 3 numbers with 1 or 2 decimal places.

? What if the order of the digits was 1 to 9?

Let's practise

1 Copy each multiplication.
Which do you think has the answer nearest to 1000?
Approximate first, then find each exact answer.

a $112 \times 42 = \square$ **b** $217 \times 35 = \square$ **c** $328 \times 37 = \square$

d $431 \times 46 = \square$ **e** $535 \times 63 = \square$ **f** $638 \times 47 = \square$

2 On the banks of the Nile, Ancient Egyptians are measuring their fields.
Find the area of each field.

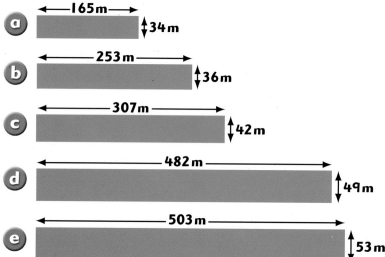

a 165 m × 34 m

b 253 m × 36 m

c 307 m × 42 m

d 482 m × 49 m

e 503 m × 53 m

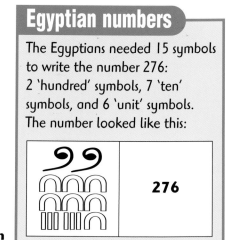

Egyptian numbers

The Egyptians needed 15 symbols to write the number 276:
2 'hundred' symbols, 7 'ten' symbols, and 6 'unit' symbols.
The number looked like this:

276

Let's investigate

3 Callum used the digits   2   4   6   7   8   to complete this multiplication.

$472 \times 68 = 32\,096$

Investigate different 3-digit by 2-digit products using the same digits.
Which product gives the largest answer?
Which product gives the smallest answer?

? What if the product was 4-digit by 1-digit?
Use the same digits as in question 3.

$\square\ \square\ \square\ \square\ \times\ \square$

Let's practise

1 **a** Copy and complete.

$9 \times 9 + 7 = \square$
$98 \times 9 + 6 = \square$
$987 \times 9 + 5 = \square$
$9876 \times 9 + 4 = \square$
$98\,765 \times 9 + 3 = \square$

b Write about any patterns you notice.

c Predict the answers to

- $987\,654 \times 9 + 2$
- $9\,876\,543 \times 9 + 1$

Check your predictions.

2 **a** Copy and complete.

$1{\cdot}2 \times 9 + 0{\cdot}3 = \square$
$12{\cdot}3 \times 9 + 0{\cdot}4 = \square$
$123{\cdot}4 \times 9 + 0{\cdot}5 = \square$
$1234{\cdot}5 \times 9 + 0{\cdot}6 = \square$
$12\,345{\cdot}6 \times 9 + 0{\cdot}7 = \square$

b Write about any patterns you notice.

c Predict the answer to

- $123\,456{\cdot}7 \times 9 + 0{\cdot}8$

Check your prediction.

Let's investigate

3 Investigate arranging the digits to complete this multiplication.

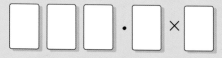

$$\boxed{}\boxed{}\boxed{}{\cdot}\boxed{} \times \boxed{}$$

What is the largest possible answer?
What is the smallest possible answer?

? What if the multiplication was  ?

Isaac Newton (1642–1727)

One of Newton's most famous achievements was demonstrating the law of gravity after observing an apple fall from a tree. When asked how he solved such significant problems, he allegedly replied: 'By always thinking about them ... I keep the subject of my inquiry constantly before me, and wait till the first dawning opens gradually ... into a full and clear light.'

DONK!

Let's practise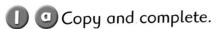

1 **a** Copy and complete.

158·73 × 2 × 7 = ☐

158·73 × 3 × 7 = ☐

158·73 × 5 × 7 = ☐

158·73 × 9 × 7 = ☐

b Write about any patterns you notice.

c Predict and check the answers to:

- 158·73 × 4 × 7 = ☐
- 158·73 × 6 × 7 = ☐
- 158·73 × 7 × 7 = ☐

> ### The metric system
>
> The use of decimals has become much more important and common since the introduction of the metric system of money and measurement.
>
> Britain adopted the metric system of money in 1971, almost 200 years after it was first used in France in the 1790s, during the French Revolution. France officially adopted the use of decimal money in 1799.

2 Do not use a calculator. Use the multiplications in question 1 to find:

a 1587·3 × 2 x 7 = ☐

b 15·873 × 5 × 7 = ☐

c 158·73 × 14 = ☐

d 1·5873 × 21 = ☐

e 158·73 × 42 = ☐

f 15·873 × 63 = ☐

g 1·5873 × 49 = ☐

h 0·15873 × 28 = ☐

Let's investigate

3 Investigate the multiplication

1·43 × ☐ × 7

where the empty box contains any one of the digits 1 to 9.

? What if the multiplication was

14·3 × ☐ × 7?

Let's practise 🖩

1 Copy and complete, calculating mentally. Approximate first.

a 381 ÷ 4 = ☐ **b** 456 ÷ 4 = ☐ **c** 482 ÷ 5 = ☐ **d** 531 ÷ 5 = ☐

e 674 ÷ 5 = ☐ **f** 629 ÷ 8 = ☐ **g** 815 ÷ 8 = ☐ **h** 987 ÷ 8 = ☐

Check your answers using a calculator.

Let's solve problems

2 **a** 6 chocolate bars cost £2·34.
How much does 1 bar cost?

b Joanna and her 6 friends have £9·94 between
them. They share it equally.
How much does each get?

c Jack delivered a total of 648 newspapers
during 9 paper rounds last month.
He delivered the same number of newspapers
on each round. How many was that?

d Denzil drove 924 km during his first week as a
salesman. He worked on 6 days. What was the
mean distance he drove each day?

e Denzil's boss thought that Denzil should have
covered the 924 km in 5 days. What would his
mean daily distance have been if he had?

Let's play A game for 2

- Place the cards face up.
- Players take turns to choose a card until each has 4 cards.
- Both players make a 3-digit ÷ 1-digit calculation with their 4 cards.
- Each player works out the answer to their division.
- The player with the answer nearer to 150 scores a point.
- The first to 5 points is the winner.

You need

a set of 0 to 9 cards

Let's practise

1 Use a written method to find the missing numbers.

   a 406 ÷ 7 = ☐   **b** 539 ÷ 7 = ☐   **c** 963 ÷ 9 = ☐

   d 528 ÷ ☐ = 6   **e** 592 ÷ ☐ = 8   **f** 956 ÷ ☐ = 4

2 Use a written method to find the missing numbers.

   a 390 ÷ 13 = ☐   **b** 665 ÷ 19 = ☐   **c** 962 ÷ 37 = ☐

   d 828 ÷ ☐ = 46   **e** 901 ÷ ☐ = 53   **f** 948 ÷ ☐ = 79

Let's solve problems

3 Brian, a professional weightlifter, is working out his calorie intake. Work out the quantities of the different foods he can eat to gain the calorie amounts in the table.

Calorie chart

cereal	94 per 25 g
bread	62 per slice
eggs	72 per egg
sausages	84 per sausage
cheese	99 per 25 g
potatoes	87 per 100 g

Calories	Food item	Quantity
360	eggs	**a**
372	slices of bread	**b**
588	sausages	**c**

Calories	Food item	Quantity
752	cereal portions (25 g)	**d**
594	cheese portions (25 g)	**e**
261	potato portions (100 g)	**f**

Let's practise

1 Divide these numbers by 2, 3, 4, 5 and 6.

a 65   **b** 73   **c** 83

> To 7 decimal places:
>
> $\frac{1}{6}$ is 0·166 6667
>
> $\frac{2}{6}$ or $\frac{1}{3}$ is 0·333 3333
>
> $\frac{4}{6}$ or $\frac{2}{3}$ is 0·666 6667
>
> $\frac{5}{6}$ is 0·833 3333

Let's solve problems

2 Look at the boxes of blank CDs.

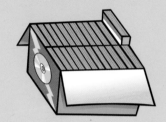

Box of 15 CDs
£24·45

Box of 25 CDs
£33·75

Box of 38 CDs
plus 2 extra free
£57·60

a Find the cost of one CD in each pack.

b Find different ways of buying 40 CDs. What does each cost?

c Find different ways of buying 65 CDs. What does each cost?

d Find different ways of buying 80 CDs. What does each cost?

Let's play   **A game for 2**

You need

a dice

- Player 1 says a number between 50 and 100, e.g. 73.
- Player 2 rolls the dice, divides player 1's number by the dice number and says the answer aloud, e.g. 73 ÷ 4 = 18·25
- Player 1 checks with a calculator.
- If correct, player 2 scores:
  - ◆ 0 for a whole-number answer
  - ◆ 1 for a decimal answer with 1 decimal place
  - ◆ 2 for a decimal answer with 2 decimal places
  - ◆ 3 for a decimal answer with more than 2 decimal places.
- Change roles so that player 2 says a number and player 1 rolls the dice.

The first player with 10 points wins.

Let's solve problems

1 A lorry delivers food to local shops. The lists show how much of each item is on the lorry. The amounts are shared equally between the shops.

How much of each item does each shop get?

a
5 shops
47·5 kg sugar
67·5 kg flour
6·25 kg salt
78·5 kg apples
71·5 l milk

b
8 shops
46·4 kg tea
87·2 kg flour
146·8 kg potatoes
169·2 kg meat
250·4 l milk

2

55·04	42·48	105·28
117·84	67·6	17·36
29·92	92·72	80·16

13·76		

a The first grid above is a 'magic square'.
What is the total of each row, column or diagonal?

b Complete the second grid by dividing each number in the magic square by 4.
What is the total of each row, column or diagonal in the new grid?
Explain why this grid is also a magic square.

Let's investigate

3 Investigate arranging the digits to complete this division.

2   4   8
   3   7

What is the largest possible answer?
What is the smallest possible answer?

? What if the division was:

 ?

Dangerous designs

John Napier, credited for introducing modern decimal notation, also created early designs for the submarine, tank and machine gun. However, he was so horrified by the potential destruction that could be caused by these machines that he destroyed his designs.

Let's solve problems

① Use a written method to answer these questions.

ⓐ The area of a rectangle is 435 cm².
Its width is 15 cm. What is its length?

ⓑ A secret number is multiplied by 47.
The answer is 893.
What is the secret number?

ⓒ A coach makes the same trip 18 times in a week.
At the end of the week it has travelled 936 miles.
What is the length of each trip?

ⓓ I think of a number, multiply it by 78 and the answer is 858.
What is my number?

Code breaking

The Enigma coding machine had a crucial flaw that helped code-breakers to crack the code: letters in the original message never appeared as the same letter in code.

② Find which letter stands for which digit in each division calculation.

ⓐ
$$\begin{array}{r} AC \\ AB \overline{)ADC} \end{array}$$
The digits are 1, 2, 6 and 9.

ⓑ
$$\begin{array}{r} DC \\ AB \overline{)CAB} \end{array}$$
The digits are 1, 2, 3 and 5.

ⓒ
$$\begin{array}{r} DC \\ AB \overline{)CCC} \end{array}$$
The digits are 1, 2, 3 and 7.

Let's play A game for 2

- Both players choose a number from each box to make a division.
- Keep a record of the numbers that are selected. They cannot be used again.
- Record your division and write an approximate answer.
- Use a calculator to find the exact answer.
- A point is scored by the player whose approximation is closer to their exact answer.

The first to score 3 points wins.

338	676	390	225
195	462	551	
754	255	221	

13	26	22	39	15
33	28	48	59	
52	17	44		

Let's solve problems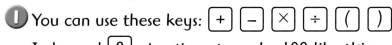

1 You can use these keys: $\boxed{+}$ $\boxed{-}$ $\boxed{\times}$ $\boxed{\div}$ $\boxed{(}$ $\boxed{)}$

Jade used $\boxed{8}$ nine times to make 100 like this:

$\boxed{8}$ $\boxed{8}$ $\boxed{+}$ $\boxed{8}$ $\boxed{+}$ $\boxed{(}$ $\boxed{8}$ $\boxed{+}$ $\boxed{8}$ $\boxed{)}$ $\boxed{\div}$ $\boxed{8}$ $\boxed{+}$ $\boxed{(}$ $\boxed{8}$ $\boxed{+}$ $\boxed{8}$ $\boxed{)}$ $\boxed{\div}$ $\boxed{8}$

Make 100: **a** Use $\boxed{9}$ four times.   **b** Use $\boxed{4}$ seven times.

        c Use $\boxed{5}$ five times.   **d** Use $\boxed{3}$ five times.

        e Use $\boxed{6}$ eight times.

2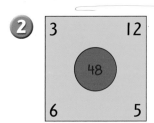

3		12
	48	
6		5

> To calculate the number in the circle you find the sum of the top left and the bottom right numbers, and multiply this by the difference between the bottom left and top right numbers.

a
3		23
11		6

b
38		12
35		29

c
29		58
28		47

Let's investigate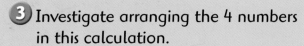

3 Investigate arranging the 4 numbers in this calculation.

$\boxed{137}$ $\boxed{473}$ $\boxed{289}$ $\boxed{378}$

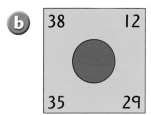

$(\ \boxed{} + \boxed{}\ ) \times (\ \boxed{} + \boxed{}\ ) =$

> Don't forget to work out the parts in the brackets first!

What is the smallest possible answer?

What is the largest possible answer?

? What if the calculation was

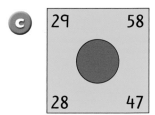

$(\ \boxed{} - \boxed{}\ ) \times (\ \boxed{} - \boxed{}\ ) = ?$

Let's practise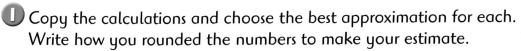

1 Copy the calculations and choose the best approximation for each.
Write how you rounded the numbers to make your estimate.

a	23 × 56	**128**	**1288**	**12 888**
b	387 × 9	**3483**	**348**	**34 832**
c	465 × 78	**3627**	**362 700**	**36 270**
d	3402 ÷ 54	**63**	**6·3**	**630**
e	18 598 ÷ 34	**5470**	**547**	**54·7**
f	30 258 ÷ 82	**3690**	**36·9**	**369**

Now check each answer using the inverse operation.
Do not use a calculator.

2 Choose 2 of these numbers to make a multiplication.

356	497	718	603

Predict whether the answer will be odd or even.
Now check your answer. Do this 5 times.

Let's solve problems

3 Answer each question without doing the full calculation.

a Sam buys 5 items costing £1·23, 85p, 64p, £2·31 and 78p.
He pays with a £10 note and gets £4·25 change.
He knows immediately this is wrong. How?

b Mel works out how many 26p stamps she can buy for £5.
Her answer is 30.
Explain how you know she is wrong.

c Sunil's bill has prices £5·43, 37p, £2·54, £2·02 and 99p.
He pays with a £20 note and gets £10·65 change.
He knows immediately this is wrong. How?

d Ali works out £3·51 plus 49p on a calculator.
The display shows £52·51. Where has Ali gone wrong?

? What if I think of a number, multiply it by 27 and subtract 1?
The answer is odd. Is the number I am thinking of odd or even?
How do you know?

Let's practise

1 Copy, replacing each ⬤ with **+, −, x, ÷** or **=**.

    a) 810 ⬤ 135 ⬤ 9 ⬤ 54   b) 16 875 ⬤ 25 ⬤ 810 ⬤ 135

    c) 810 ⬤ 135 ⬤ 50 300 ⬤ 59 050   d) 810 ⬤ 135 ⬤ 954 ⬤ 9

Let's solve problems

2 Find which letter stands for which digit in each multiplication.

    a) SR × PQ = RPQ   The digits are 1, 2, 3 and 5.

    b) PR × PQ = PSR   The digits are 1, 2, 6 and 9.

3 a) Find 3 consecutive numbers with a product of 54 834.

    b) Find 3 consecutive odd numbers with a product of 12 075.

    c) Find 3 consecutive square numbers with a product of 14 400.

    d) Find 3 consecutive prime numbers with a product of 7429.

Let's investigate

4 a) Jasmine used the digits 0 to 9, in order, to make 100.
     Use addition and subtraction signs to make her statement correct

     | 1 | 2 | 3 | 4 | 5 | 6 | 7 | 8 | 9 | = 100

    b) How many ways can you make 100 by adding and subtracting the same digits in order?

      ● How close to 100 can you get?

      ● Can you make 100 exactly?

? What if you reversed the order of the digits? What if you used muliplication signs as well?

Let's solve problems

1 Eight schools were each given 75 free children's tickets to a charity medieval fair. Each child's ticket normally costs £4·75.

  a How many pounds' worth of tickets were given away free?

  b 489 of the free tickets were used at the fair.
How many were not used?

At the fair twice as many children paid for a ticket as had a free ticket.

  c How many children paid for a ticket?

  d How many children were there at the fair?

There were 12 406 adults and children at the fair.
3494 of the adults were men.

  e How many women were at the fair?

There were no free tickets for adults. Adults paid £15·00 each.

  f How much money was collected for all the adult tickets?

  g How much money was collected for all the tickets, including the children who paid?

£2385·93 was spent on refreshments at the fair and 3 times as much as that was spent on souvenirs.

  h How much money was spent in total, including tickets, souvenirs and refreshments?

  i How much was spent on average by each person at the fair?

2 Jeremy and Jennie are going on holiday.
Jeremy changed £175 to euros on May 12th.
Jennie changed the same amount on May 19th.

  a Who has more euros?

  b How many more?

	Exchange rate
May 12th	£1 = 1·61 euros
May 19th	£1 = 1·54 euros

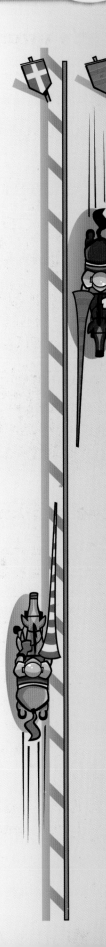

Let's solve problems 🖩

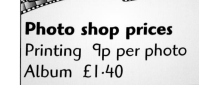

PHOTO SHOP

Photo shop prices
Printing 9p per photo
Album £1·40

① Kevin went to the photo shop and paid
a total of £5·09 for an album and his photos.
How many photos did he collect?

② The cost of a £12 000 car decreased by 15% in
April but then increased by 10% in September.
What was the price of the car at the end of September?

③ Five friends went bowling. The cost was £22.
How much would it cost 8 people to go bowling?

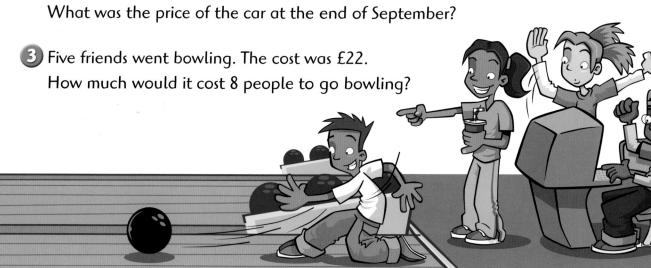

④ Lucy wants to buy a new car costing £8500.
The dealer offers her £2236 in part-exchange for her old car.

ⓐ How much extra does she need?

ⓑ She decides to borrow this amount and pay it back in equal
monthly amounts of £174. For how many months will she
have to pay this?

⑤ A builder works at £12 per hour for 28 hours
and £15 per hour for 9 hours.
How much does he earn in the 37 hours?

⑥ £1 = 2·5 Australian dollars.
How much is £1·50 in Australian dollars?

⑦ A 1kg box of nuts costs £3·50.
Each nut has a mass of 20 g.
How much does each nut cost?

Money

Australia started using decimal money
(dollars and cents) in 1966.

Let's practise

1 Write each expression using letter symbols.

a a number add 3

b 7 add a number

c 10 minus a number

d a number subtract 4

e multiply a number by 3 and add 2

f a number divided by 4

g a number multiplied by 5 and 8 subtracted

h 9 divided by a number

i a number squared

j a number minus 4 and then multiplied by 2

Algebra

The first recorded use of algebra in Britain was in the 16th century, but it had been in use in the Middle East for many centuries before.

The major work of the 9th century Arab al-Khowarizmi was entitled *Al-jabr wa'lmugabalah*, meaning 'restoration and balance'. It is from the first word in this title than we have the word 'algebra'.

2 Write each expression in words.

a $n + 10$ **b** $4n - 1$ **c** $2n + 3$

d $6a$ **e** $\frac{b}{3}$ **f** $5 - c$

g $3n - 2$ **h** $3(n - 2)$ **i** $3n - 6$

Let's investigate

3 • This is a magic square.

Find the sum of the 3 expressions in each row, column and diagonal using letter symbols.

This sum is called the magic number.

• Investigate making magic squares using different values of x, y and z.

What is the magic number of each square you make?

$x - z$	$x + y + z$	$x - y$
$x - y + z$	x	$x + y - z$
$x + y$	$x - y - z$	$x + z$

? What if the magic number was 12?
Find different sets of values for x, y and z.

Let's solve problems

1 In a triangular arithmagon the number in each square box is the sum of the 2 numbers in the circles on each side of it.

- Copy each arithmagon below.
- Write in each missing number as an expression using *n*.
- Try to write an equation to help you find the solution for each arithmagon.

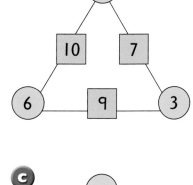

a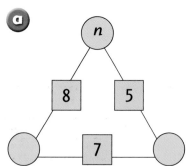

b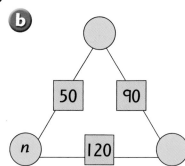

c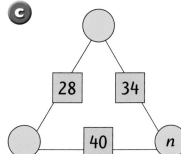

Let's investigate

2 a Investigate possible solutions to this square arithmagon.

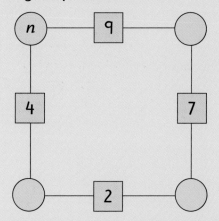

b What do you notice about the sum of the 4 corner numbers?

? What if the arithmagon was a pentagon with the numbers 3, 5, 12, 13, 7 in the square boxes?

Let's practise

1 Use letters and numbers to write each formula.
Explain what each letter you use represents.

a number of minutes = 60 times the number of hours

b age in years = age in months divided by twelve

c area of a triangle = one half the product of the height and the base

d distance travelled = speed multiplied by time

2 Copy and complete each table.
Write about a possible meaning for each formula.

a

A = lw		
l	w	A
3	7	
9	5	
8	12	
6		72
	11	55

b

m = c ÷ 100	
m	c
2	
	450
7·25	
10·5	
	1085

c

p = 2l + 2w		
l	w	p
8	4	
12	6	
7	5	
5		26
	9	30

Let's solve problems

3 Write each puzzle as an equation.
Use *n* to represent the secret number.
Solve each equation.

a I think of a secret number,
add 7 and my answer is 12.

b I think of a secret number,
subtract 15 and my answer is 15.

c I think of a secret number,
multiply it by 3 and my answer is 12.

d I think of a secret number,
divide it by 7 and my answer is 4.

e I think of a secret number,
multiply it by 5 and add 2 and my answer is 12.

Robert Recorde (1510–1558)

The Frenchman Recorde introduced the equals sign '=' in 1557 because he thought that no 2 things could be more equal than 2 parallel lines of the same length.

Let's solve problems

1 This is the start of a sequence of squares.

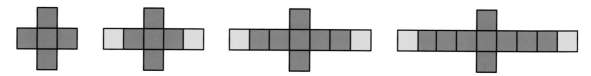

a Copy and complete the table.

Shape number (n)	1	2	3	4	5	6	7	8
Number of squares (s)	5	7						

b Write a formula that connects n and s.

2 This is the start of a sequence of triangles and rectangles.

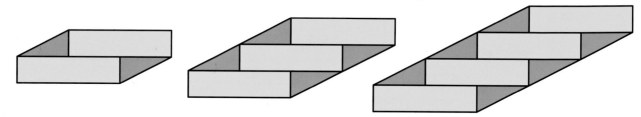

a Copy and complete the table.

Number of rectangles (R)	2	3	4	5	6	7	8	9
Number of triangles (T)	2	4						

b Write a formula that connects R and T.

Let's investigate

3 The solution to the equation $10 + \blacksquare\, y = 8 + \blacktriangle\, y$ is $y = 2$.

Investigate the values of the missing numbers $\blacksquare$ and $\blacktriangle$.

? What if the solution to the equation was $y = \frac{1}{2}$?

Let's practise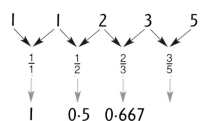

1 Each sequence uses the same rule.

Copy and continue each sequence until you have 15 numbers in each one.

a 1, 1, 2, 3, 5, 8, 13...   **b** 3, 6, 9, 15, 24, 39, 63...

c 4, ⁻1, 3, 2, 5, 7, 12...   **d** ⁻2, 0, ⁻2, ⁻2, ⁻4, ⁻6, ⁻10...

Sequences with the rule 'add the previous 2 numbers' are called Fibonacci sequences.

2 **a** Copy the sequence and complete the calculations below.

Use a calculator and write the decimals to the nearest thousandth.

1   1   2   3   5   8   13   21   34   55

$\frac{1}{1}$ $\frac{1}{2}$ $\frac{2}{3}$ $\frac{3}{5}$

1   0·5   0·667

b Write about what is happening in the decimal number sequence.

Let's investigate

3 Here is the best-known Fibonacci sequence written in a table.

F(1)	F(2)	F(3)	F(4)	F(5)	F(6)	F(7)	F(8)	F(9)	F(10)
1	1	2	3	5	8	13	21	34	55

a Calculate:

- $F(1) + F(2) + F(3) + F(4) + F(5) + F(6) + F(7) + F(8) + F(9) + F(10)$
- $11 \times F(7)$

b Write about what you notice.

c Investigate other Fibonacci sequences to see if the same relationship is true.

Fibonacci (1170–1250)

Leonardo Pisano, otherwise known as Fibonacci, wrote the book *Liber abaci* in 1202. The book covered many mathematical problems that he had accumulated in his travels abroad, one of which was the 1, 1, 2, 3, 5... sequence.

Let's practise

1 Write each sequence to 8 terms. **a** 1st term: 7 rule: + 4 **b** 1st term: $\frac{1}{9}$ rule: × 3

Let's investigate

You need

interlocking cubes, squared paper

2 **a** Make the first shapes in the L sequence up to L(7).

L(1)   L(2)   L(3)

b Copy and complete the table.

Shape	L(1)	L(2)	L(3)	L(4)	L(5)	L(6)	L(7)
Value (number of cubes)	3	5					

c Predict the value of L(10) and L(20). Check by making the shapes.

3 • Copy each sequence on squared paper and extend it for 4 more steps.
• Draw a table of the number of each shape and its value.
• Predict the values of T(25), X(52), C(100).

a T sequence: **b** X sequence: **c** C sequence:

T(1)   X(1)   C(1)

T(2)   X(2)    C(2)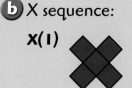

4 Meg writes the first 2 terms of a sequence: 3   8
She asks Kelly and Greg to guess the rule and continue the sequence.

Kelly's rule: +5   Kelly's sequence   3, 8, 13, 18, 23, 28

Greg's rule: × 3 – 1 Greg's sequence   3, 8, 23, 68, 203, 608

Who is right, Kelly or Greg? Write about your findings.

Investigate other rules for sequences that start 3, 8... Use at least 4 terms.

Let's practise

1 Write a function for each.

IN → | function: $n \rightarrow$ | → OUT

a

IN	OUT
4	6
3	5
20	22
15	17

$n \rightarrow$

b

IN	OUT
1	3
9	27
3	9
10	30

$n \rightarrow$

c

IN	OUT
6	10
4	6
7	12
10	18

$n \rightarrow$

d

IN	OUT
1	8
4	14
2	10
5	16

$n \rightarrow$

e

IN	OUT
4	16
1	1
5	25
10	100

$n \rightarrow$

Let's solve problems

2 ● Draw each sequence on squared paper.

● Extend the sequence for 3 more terms.

● Write a function to find the nth term in the sequence.

You need

squared paper

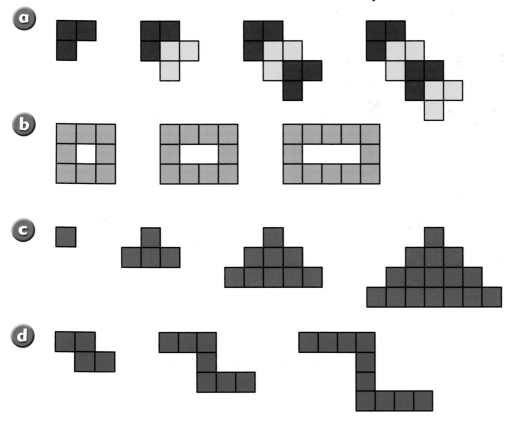

a

b

c

d

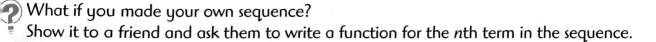

? What if you made your own sequence?
Show it to a friend and ask them to write a function for the nth term in the sequence.

Let's practise

1 Copy the coordinate pairs. Complete the rule.

a (3, 5), (7, 9), (1, 3), (10, 12)

rule: $x + \boxed{} = y$

b (6, 13), (⁻2, 5), (1, 8), (⁻8, ⁻1)

rule: $x + \boxed{} = y$

c (2, ⁻4), (⁻3, ⁻9), (6, 0), (0, ⁻6)

rule: $x - \boxed{} = y$

d (4, ⁻6), (10, 0), (12, 2), (⁻1, ⁻11)

rule: $x - \boxed{} = y$

2 Write the rule for each graph.

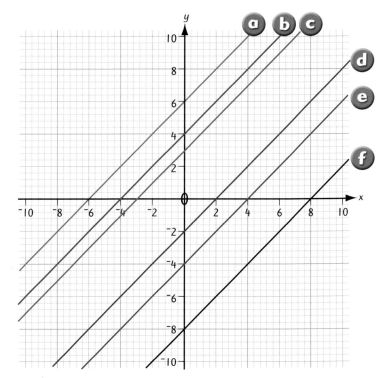

Let's investigate

You need

graph paper

3 ● Draw the x-axis and the y-axis from ⁻10 to +10.
  ● Draw the graph of the line $x + 1 = y$.
  ● Write the coordinates of the point where $x + 1 = y$ crosses the y-axis.
  ● Predict the coordinates of the point where the line $x + 2 = y$ crosses the y-axis.
    Test your prediction by drawing the graph of the line $x + 2 = y$.
  ● Investigate the coordinates of the points where the lines
    $x + 4 = y$, $x - 7 = y$, $x + 6 = y$ and $x - 2 = y$ cross the y-axis.
  ● Write a general statement about the rules for these lines and where they
    cross the y-axis.

Let's practise

1 Copy the coordinate pairs. Complete the rule.

a (4, 20), (7, 35), (2, 10), (6, 30)

    rule: ☐ x = y

b (5, 45), (10, 90), (1, 9), (3, 27)

    rule: ☐ x = y

c (8, 56), (11, 77), (4, 28), (9, 63)

    rule: ☐ x = y

2 Write the rule for each graph.

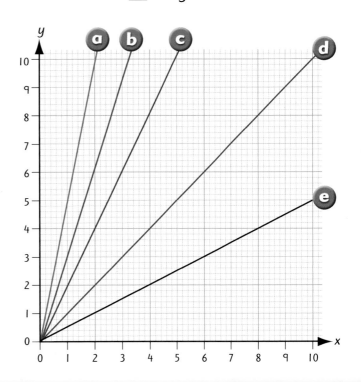

René Descartes (1596–1650)

Descartes gave his name to Cartesian coordinates: a system whereby the position of a point on a graph or a map is given by its distance from 2 lines, named x and y.

Let's investigate

You need

graph paper, a protractor

3
- Draw x- and y-axes from 0 to 10.
- Draw the graph of the line x = y.
- Measure the angle between the line x = y and the x-axis.
- Predict the angle that the line 2x = y will make with the x-axis.
- Test your prediction by drawing the graph of the line 2x = y.
- Investigate the angle that the lines 3x = y, 4x = y, 5x = y... make with the x-axis.
- Write a general statement about the lines and the angle they make with the x-axis.

Let's practise

1 ● Draw *x*- and *y*-axes from ⁻5 to 5 on graph paper.

● In blue, draw graphs of the lines $y = x$, $y = x - 3$ and $y = x + 5$.

● In red, draw graphs of the lines $y = {}^-x$, $y = {}^-3 - x$ and $y = 5 - x$.

● Label each graph with its equation.

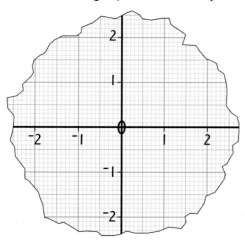

Hypatia of Alexandria (c.370–415)

Hypatia is the first known of many women who have influenced mathematics over the ages. Remarkably for a woman of her time, she became a professor of mathematics at the University of Alexandria. However, her education and great mind scared the population of Alexandria, many of whom thought they were only suitable for a man. This fear may have been one reason that led to her cruel murder in 415.

a Write about the slope of the 3 blue graphs.

b What in the equations $y = x$, $y = x - 3$ and $y = x + 5$ tells you that the graphs will be parallel lines?

c What are the coordinates of the points where each graph crosses the *x*-axis and the *y*-axis?

2 Repeat questions **1a**, **1b** and **1c** for the red graphs.

Let's investigate

3 **a** Use the same scale on both axes to draw the graphs of $y = 2x$ and $y = {}^-\frac{1}{2}x$.

b Write what you notice about the 2 lines.

c Investigate finding other pairs of lines that cross at right angles.

Let's practise

1

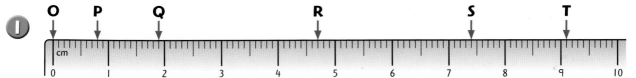

Write the length of OP, PQ, QR, RS and ST in centimetres,
in millimetres and in metres.

2 The gardeners at MacKinnon Castle are cleaning the gardening tools.
Write the measurements of each garden tool in millimetres.

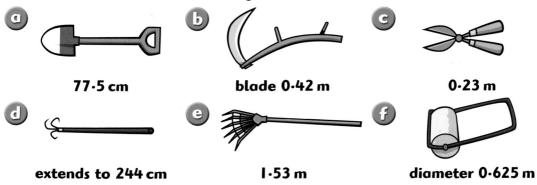

a 77·5 cm

b blade 0·42 m

c 0·23 m

d extends to 244 cm

e 1·53 m

f diameter 0·625 m

Let's solve problems 🖩

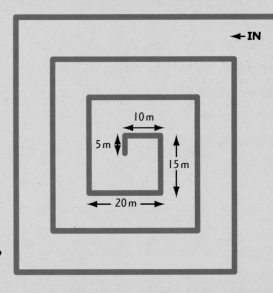

3 The lawn is mown weekly.
One gardener trims the edges after each mowing.

  a Find the total distance he trims after one
     mowing.

  b How many kilometres of lawn edge does
     he trim in a season of 26 weeks?

4 There is a spiral maze. Beginning at
the centre, the length of a side of the
hedge increases by 5 m each time.

  a Find the total length of hedge in the maze.

  b A gardener can trim 48 m of hedge in
     a day. Work out how long it takes him to
     trim all the hedge in the maze.

  c If 2 gardeners are employed, the hedge
     can be trimmed in 5 days.
     What length of hedge is trimmed each day?

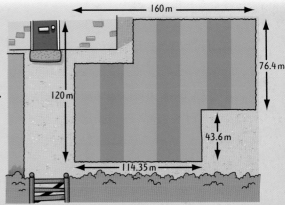

Let's solve problems

1 Dennis has a DIY store.

On Saturday his first customer bought $\frac{1}{3}$ of a roll of chicken wire.

A second customer bought $\frac{1}{3}$ of the remainder.

A third customer bought $\frac{1}{3}$ of the wire that was left.

A fourth customer asked for 10 m of chicken wire.

'Sorry,' said Dennis, 'There's only 8 m left.'

How many metres of chicken wire did

Dennis have at the start of the day?

2 Dennis has a roll of narrow tape 32 m long.

He folds it in half to cut it, then in half again and notes:

Fold	0	1	2
Number of pieces	1	2	4
Length of each piece	32 m	16 m	8 m

Metre

The word 'metre' comes from the Greek word 'metron' meaning 'to measure'.

a How many pieces of tape will he have if he continues to fold it in half and to cut it 4 more times?

b What is the length of each piece of tape?

3 Liam's house is 406 m from Dennis's DIY store.

There is a lamp-post outside his house, and another in front of the DIY store. There are 6 more in between.

All 8 lamp-posts are the same distance apart.

How far apart are:

a the first and third lamp-posts

b the second and fifth lamp-posts

c the third and eighth lamp-posts?

4 Not counting the covers, Dennis's stockbook is 20 mm thick. The pages are numbered 1 to 398.

Find the thickness of 1 sheet of paper in his book.

Let's solve problems

2·5 cm ≈ 1 inch
30 cm ≈ 1 foot
8 km ≈ 5 miles

1 A shop buys candles from France and candlesticks from the USA.

475 mm	**60 cm**	**0·125 m**	**25 inches**	**10 inches**	**1 foot**

Made in France   *Made in USA*

- Choose a candle and a candlestick.
- Find their approximate total height in cm.
- Repeat for all 9 combinations of a candle and a candlestick.

475 mm + 25 inches

≈ 47·5 cm + (25 × 2·5) cm

≈ 47·5 cm + 62·5 cm

≈ 110 cm

2 This function machine converts miles to kilometres, giving an approximate answer.

miles → | **×8** > → | **÷5** > → km

Convert these distances from Perth into kilometres. Round your answers to the nearest kilometre.

Distances from Perth

Dundee	21 miles
Edinburgh	41 miles
Glasgow	57 miles
London	416 miles
Stirling	33 miles
Oxford	390 miles

3 This function machine converts kilometres to miles, approximately.

km → | **×5** > → | **÷8** > → mile

Convert these distances from Oxford into miles. Round your answers to the nearest mile.

Distances from Oxford

Cardiff	170 km
London	91 km
Manchester	230 km
Newcastle	416 km
Nottingham	157 km
Perth	624 km

Let's practise

The Royal Mint regulates the mass of UK coins. Every coin of the same value has exactly the same mass when minted.

| 12 g | 9·5 g | 8·0 g | 5·0 g | 6·5 g | 3·25 g | 7·12 g | 3·56 g |

1 What is the total value of:

  a 1 kg in 20p coins

  b 0·48 kg in £2 coins

  c 0·48 kg in 50p coins

  d 0·95 kg in £1 coins?

Let's solve problems

2 Brenda paid in 8 bags of coins at the bank.
Find the total mass in grams of each bag of coins.

  a £20 in £2 coins

  b £20 in £1 coins

  c £10 in 50p coins

  d £10 in 20p coins

  e £5 in 10p coins

  f £5 in 5p coins

  g £1 in 2p coins

  h £1 in 1p coins

> Remember:
> 30 g ≈ 1 oz
> 1 kg ≈ 2·2 lb

3 Find the approximate mass, to the nearest whole ounce, of each of the 8 bags of coins in question 2.

4 Ben balanced his pet cat against some bronze coins.
If his cat balanced £25, what was its mass:

  a in kilograms

  b in pounds?

5 Sally saved 3·9 kg in 10p and 5p coins.
She paid £15 in 10p coins and the rest in 5p coins into the bank.

  a What is the value of the 5p coins?

  b Last month she banked 2·2 lb of 20p coins. How much did she bank?

  c How much has she saved altogether?

Let's solve problems

1 The scales shows the mass of treats that the average British child eats in a year.

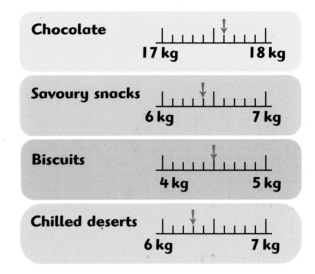

Chocolate — 17 kg | 18 kg

Savoury snacks — 6 kg | 7 kg

Biscuits — 4 kg | 5 kg

Chilled deserts — 6 kg | 7 kg

a Read the scales and work out the average total mass for all 4 treats.

b How many tonnes of savoury snacks do 1000 children eat on average in a year?

c Find the total mass in tonnes of treats eaten on average by a class of 30 children in a year.

2 a How many 10 g bars of chocolate are equivalent to 17·6 kg?

b The fat content of a 100 g chocolate bar is about 15%. What is the approximate fat content in 17·6 kg of chocolate, in grams?

3 To encourage healthy eating, a school displayed these figures for each item on its lunch menu.

Which food item has approximately:

a 25% fat

b 10% fat

c 20% fat?

Main course	Amount of fat in 85 g serving
Cod – fried in batter	9 g
Pork chop – grilled	6 g
Roast chicken	12 g
Beefburger	18 g
Sausages	21 g

4 a How many 140 g servings can the cook make from a 4·2 kg bag of potatoes?

b Work out the fat content if all the potatoes in the bag are served as:
- chips
- roast potatoes
- baked potatoes.

Potatoes	Amount of fat in 140 g serving
Chips	17 g
Roast	8 g
Baked	0·1 g

5 a Calculate the fat content in grams of the 150 g tub of yogurt.

b If you eat a tub of this yogurt at lunch each school day, how many grams of fat do you consume in 4 school weeks?

NUTRITIONAL INFORMATION

TYPICAL VALUES	PER 100 g
Energy	379 kJ (89 kcal)
Protein	4·8 g
Carbohydrate	15·6 g
Fat	1·3 g

150g ℮   Use by date on lid

Let's practise

1 **a** Copy and complete the table of values.

You need

a sheet of graph paper, a ruler

2 gallons ≈ 9 litres

Number of gallons	Number of litres
2	9
4	18
6	
8	
10	
12	

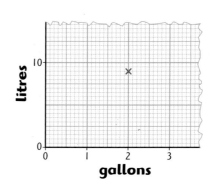

b Plot the points on graph paper.
Join them with a ruler and extend the straight line as far as it will go.

2 Use your conversion graph to convert these gallons to the nearest whole litre.

a 3 gallons   **b** 5 gallons   **c** 9 gallons   **d** 11 gallons

e 2·8 gallons   **f** 8·4 gallons   **g** 9·6 gallons   **h** 10·2 gallons

3 Use your conversion graph to convert these litres to gallons.
Write your answer to 1 decimal place.

a 10 litres   **b** 25 litres   **c** 45 litres   **d** 50 litres

e 34 litres   **f** 47 litres   **g** 12 litres   **h** 37 litres

Let's solve problems

4·5 litres ≈ 1 gallon
1 gallon = 8 pints

4 A drinks machine mixes 4 pints of syrup with 6 pints of sparkling water.
Find the amount of syrup the machine mixes with 30 gallons of water

a in pints   **b** in litres.

? What if the capacity of the syrup section of the machine was 36 litres?
How many gallons of sparkling water would be needed to make the drinks?

Let's solve problems

1 For her first experiment Dr Rennie filled ten 50 cl bottles with her secret formula. Then she placed the ten sealed bottles in an agitator crate so that no line (horizontal, vertical or diagonal) had more than 1 litre of liquid.

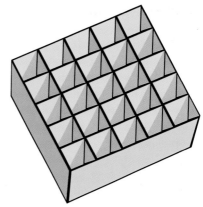

Draw a 5 x 5 square grid and show how she placed the bottles.

2 For her second experiment Dr Rennie used 2 large containers and 6 test tubes.

Show how she can pour the contents of the test tubes into the 2 containers so that there is the same amount in each container.

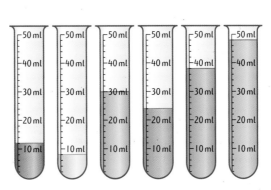

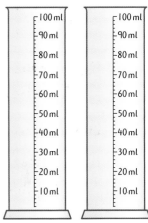

Let's investigate

3 ● Write a capacity less than 1 litre to 3 decimal places.
 ● Reverse the digits after the decimal point.
 ● Find the difference.
 ● Reverse the digits after the decimal point in the answer.
 ● Add the 2 numbers.

Dr Rennie's working

0·835 l

0·538 l

0·297 l

0·792 l

1·089 l

These results are very interesting.

Investigate other capacities using these instructions.

? What if the capacities were between 1 and 10 litres, each with 4 digits?

Let's solve problems

1 a The Olympic games first began in 776 BCE.
How many years ago is that?

b The last Ancient Olympic games was in 392 BCE.
For how many years did the games continue?

c The Ancient Olympic games were held once
every 4 years. How many games took place?

d The Modern Olympic games began in CE 1896
and are also held every 4 years.
How many years passed between the end of the
Ancient Olympic games and the beginning of the
Modern Olympic games?

e There were no Olympic games in 1916, 1940 or 1944.
How many Modern Olympic games have there been?

f How many Olympic games have there been altogether?

g The 25th Modern Olympic games were held in Barcelona, Spain in
1992. In which year are the 35th Modern Olympic games due to
be held?

2 How many days are there:

a from June 20th to August 21st inclusive

b from March 2nd to May 12th inclusive

c from December 14th to February 26th inclusive

d from October 4th to January 27th inclusive

e from July 11th to October 2nd inclusive?

3 Write 2 dates with a difference of:

a 68 days   **b** 121 days.

4 What is the date that is exactly half
way through the year?

Let's solve problems

1 It is 12:00 GMT in London. Write the local time in

a Paris   b Perth   c Moscow

d Rio de Janerio   e Edmonton   f Cape Town

g Beijing   h Lima   i Singapore   j Santiago.

2 a Work out the local time for TV viewers in these cities to watch the game live:

- San Francisco
- Nairobi
- Sydney.

EUROPEAN CUP FOOTBALL
Italy v Scotland
ROME
Kick-off 3:00pm

b At what time will the game begin for Scottish viewers?

3 The final of the Hong Kong International Rugby Sevens is at 5:30 pm local time. Write the time when the game will be screened live for rugby fans in these cities:

a London   b Perth   c Tokyo

d Wellington   e Sydney   f Johannesburg.

4 A famous painting is up for auction in New York. The auctioneer will open the telephone bidding at 12 noon New York time.

a What is the local time for a bidder phoning New York from

- Oslo   • San Francisco?

b If the local time for a bidder is 01:00 the next day, name 2 cities from which he might be calling New York.

5 A French archaeologist flies home from Mexico City. Her flight departs at 16:40 on 22nd May.

a If the flying time is 10 hours and 35 minutes, what are the date and time when her plane lands at Charles de Gaulle Airport, Paris?

b What are the time and date in Mexico City when she lands in France?

Time zones

The introduction of the railway in the late 19th century raised problems because varying local times (based on solar measurements) made it impossible to produce an accurate timetable across the country. The problem was solved by the introduction of standard time for the UK. There are now 24 time zones across the world.

Let's practise

1 Here are 3 ways to find the area of this shape.

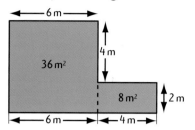
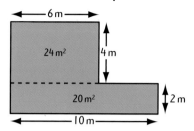
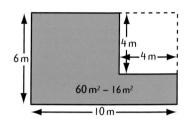

Find the area of each shape using at least 2 different ways.

a
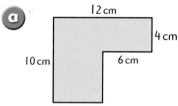

b
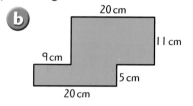

c
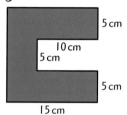

2 The orange shape is made by overlapping identical rectangles or squares. Use the formulae to work out the area and perimeter of each orange shape.

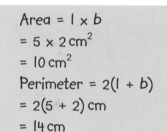

Area = l × b
= 5 × 2 cm²
= 10 cm²
Perimeter = 2(l + b)
= 2(5 + 2) cm
= 14 cm

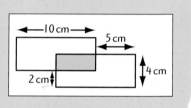

a
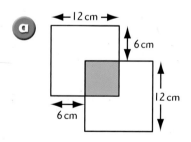

b
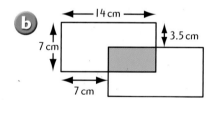

c
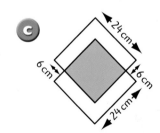

Let's solve problems

3 Fiona found the area and perimeter of 5 rectangles. Here are her results.

Find the dimensions of each rectangle.

Rectangle	a	b	c	d	e
Area	48 cm²	70 cm²	90 cm²	96 cm²	144 cm²
Perimeter	32 cm	34 cm	42 cm	56 cm	48 cm

Let's practise

You need

1 cm squared paper, ruler, scissors

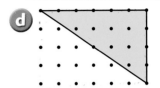

1. Work out the area of each yellow triangle in square units.

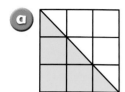 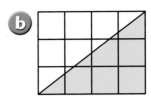 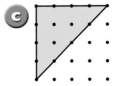

a **b** **c** **d**

2. Use the formula **area = $\frac{1}{2}$ (base × height)** to calculate the area of these right-angled triangles.

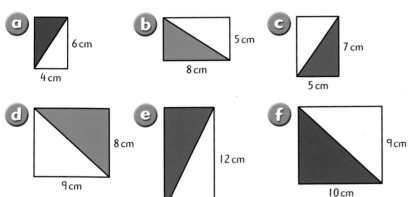

a 6 cm, 4 cm
b 5 cm, 8 cm
c 7 cm, 5 cm
d 8 cm, 9 cm
e 12 cm, 6 cm
f 9 cm, 10 cm

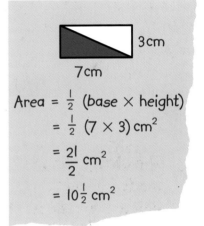

3 cm

7 cm

Area = $\frac{1}{2}$ (base × height)

= $\frac{1}{2}$ (7 × 3) cm^2

= $\frac{21}{2}$ cm^2

= $10\frac{1}{2}$ cm^2

Let's investigate

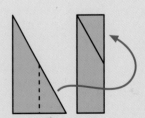

3. Ancient Greek mathematicians found the area of a right-angled triangle by changing it into a rectangle.

   a Copy each triangle on to 1 cm squared paper and cut it out.

   b Making one cut, change each triangle into a rectangle. Find its area.

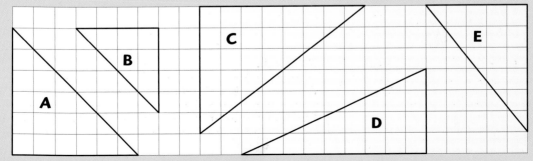

A B C D E

? What if a triangle was not right-angled?

Let's practise

1 **a** List pairs of identical shapes (there is an odd one out).

A and H

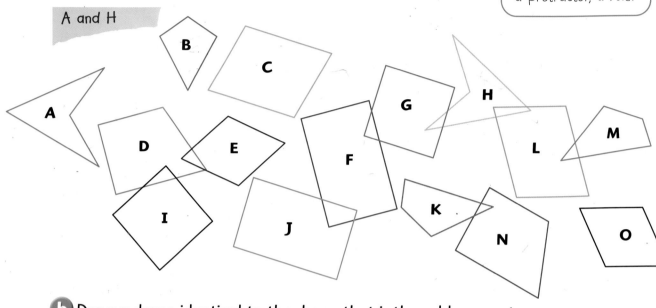

b Draw a shape identical to the shape that is the odd one out.

c Draw a pair of identical isosceles trapeziums.

d List the letters of the shapes that have at least 1 pair of parallel sides.

e List the shapes that have some perpendicular sides.

Let's solve problems

2 Follow the branches of the decision tree and write the names of the shapes that fit letters A to J.

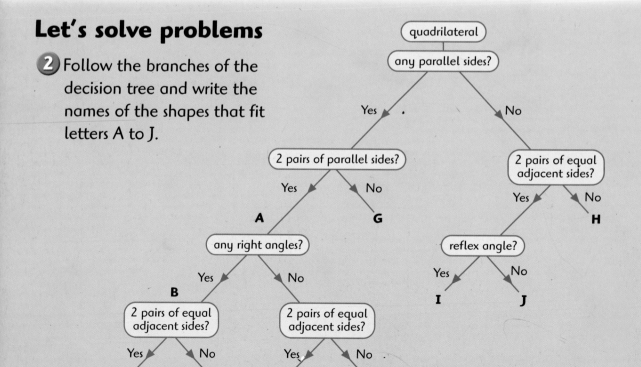

Let's practise

1 Copy and complete.

To translate shape A:

- to position B,

  add ____ units to the x-coordinates

  and ____ units to the y-coordinates.

- to position C,

  add ____ units to the x-coordinates

  and ____ units to the y-coordinates.

- to position D,

  add ____ units to the x-coordinates

  and ____ units to the y-coordinates.

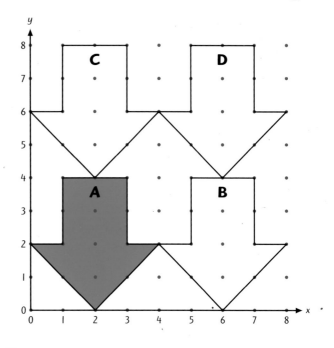

2 Write instructions to translate the red hexagon to each position A to F, in turn.

> To A: translate 2 units to the left.

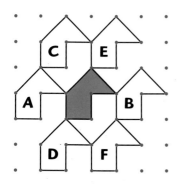

3 Find the distance and direction for each translation of the yellow quadrilateral.

> To A: translate 3 units to the left and 1 unit up.

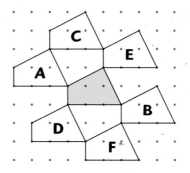

Let's investigate

4 On a 3 × 3 grid there is 1 possible translation of a 1 × 2 right-angled triangle.

Investigate possible translations of the triangle

  a on a 4 × 4 grid   **b** on a 5 × 5 grid.

? What if the triangle was a different shape?

> You need
>
> 1 cm square dotty paper

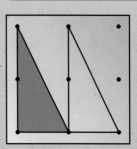

Let's investigate

You need

1cm square dotty paper, a ruler, coloured pencils

① • Copy each shape onto dotty paper.

   • Reflect each shape in the mirror line.

   • Name the resulting shape.

   • Mark equal angles and equal sides.

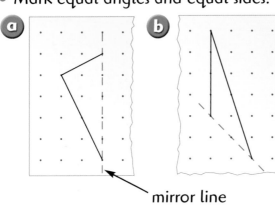 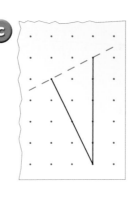 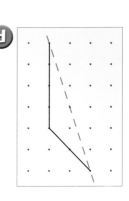

ⓐ **ⓑ** **ⓒ** **ⓓ**

mirror line

② The numbers in a magic square can be used to create symmetrical patterns.

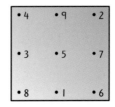 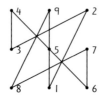

4	9	2
3	5	7
8	1	6

magic square → **3 x 3 pinboard** → **line pattern**

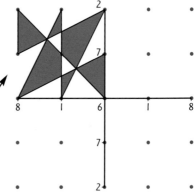

• Copy the line pattern onto 1 cm square dotty paper.

• Reflect the line pattern first horizontally and then vertically.

• Shade the pattern in the top left as shown.

• Colour the rest of the closed regions so that no 2 adjacent regions are coloured.

? What if you used these magic squares?

ⓐ

2	7	6
9	5	1
4	3	8

ⓑ

4	15	14	1
9	6	7	12
5	10	11	8
16	3	2	13

Let's investigate

You need

1 cm squared paper

1. Investigate rotating each of the shapes through 180° about the point marked with a red dot.

   Draw the original shape and its new position.

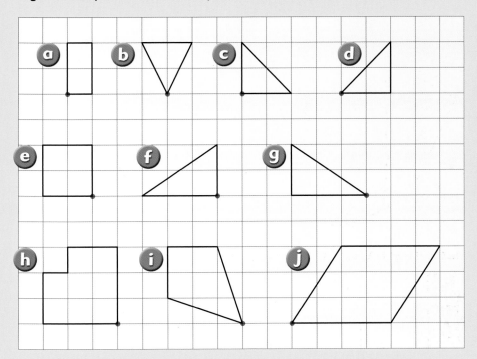

2. • Investigate rotating each shape through 180° about the given point. Draw the original shape and its new position.

   • Name the new shape formed by the rotation.

   • Mark any equal angles and any equal sides.

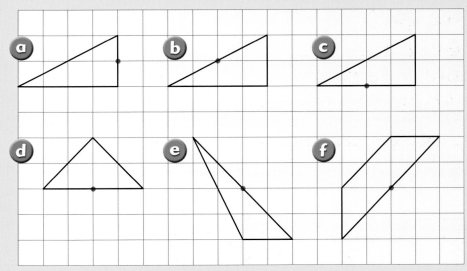

? What if you rotated the shapes in question 2 through 90° anticlockwise?

Let's practise

You can view this 3-D shape:

You need

interlocking cubes, coloured pencils, 1 cm squared paper, a ruler

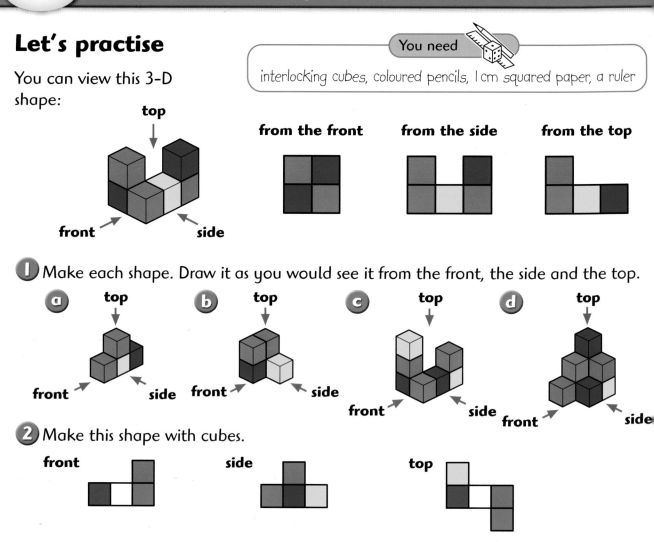

from the front **from the side** **from the top**

① Make each shape. Draw it as you would see it from the front, the side and the top.

ⓐ top ⓑ top ⓒ top ⓓ top

② Make this shape with cubes.

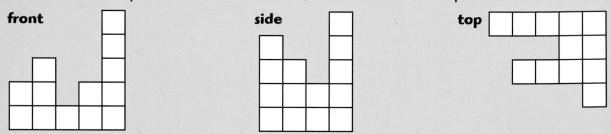

front **side** **top**

Let's investigate

③ Here is a 3-D shape shown from the front, the side and the top.

front **side** **top**

ⓐ Investigate making the shape using as many cubes as possible.

ⓑ Draw the front, side and top views showing the colours of the cubes that you used.

❓ What if you made the shape using the least number of cubes?

Let's investigate

You need

1 cm triangular dotty paper,
ruler, scissors, glue

1 Copy this net of a regular tetrahedron onto
1 cm triangular dotty paper.

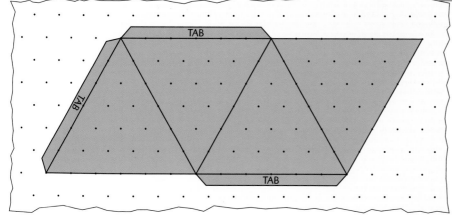

- Make 4 smaller tetrahedron nets
  with sides half as long.

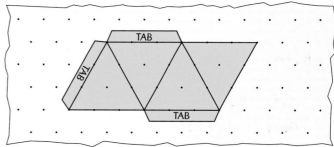

- Score along the fold lines.
  Cut and assemble all 5 tetrahedra.

- Glue each smaller tetrahedron to 1 of the faces
  of the larger tetrahedron so that the vertices of
  the smaller shape are at the midpoint of each
  edge of the larger shape.

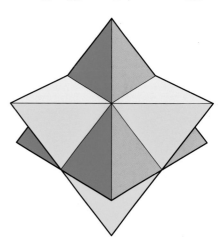

2 **a** Hold up the shape you have made and turn it
around in different directions.
Write about what you notice.

b How many vertices, edges and faces does
your shape have?

? What if you constructed other 3-D shapes
using tetrahedra?
Record and display your results.

Let's investigate

1 **a** Make a square-based pyramid:

- Draw a square with sides of 5 cm.
- Use your ruler and protractor to construct an equilateral triangle on each side of the square.
- Draw a tab on 1 edge of each triangle.
- Score the fold lines, cut out and assemble the pyramid.

b Make another identical pyramid.

c Investigate shapes that can be made by putting the 2 pyramids face to face in different ways.

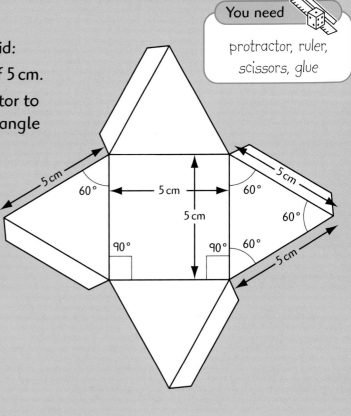

2 **a** Make a box:

- Use a ruler and protractor to construct the net.
- Score the fold lines, cut out and assemble.

b Copy and complete this sentence:

The box is a _____ prism.
It has _____ faces,
_____ edges and _____ vertices.

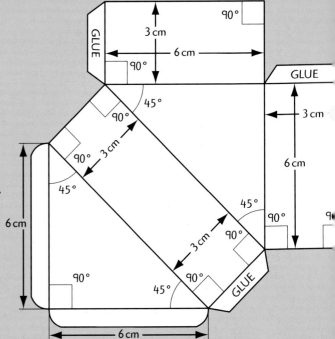

What if you looked for other nets of square-based pyramids?
How many are there?

Let's practise

1 Calculate.

a $2 \times 4 \times 16$　　**b** $4 \times 1 \times 7$

c $5 \times 5 \times 8$　　**d** $5 \times 3 \times 6$

e $6 \times 6 \times 6$　　**f** $9 \times 3 \times 3$

g $2 \times 8 \times 8$　　**h** $4 \times 8 \times 3$

i $4 \times 8 \times 4$　　**j** $9 \times 6 \times 3$

Piero della Francesca (1412–1492)

The 15th century Italian artist wrote 3 mathematical treatises including *Trattato d'abaco*.

This covered topics on algebra and the measurement of polygons and polyhedra, such as an icosahedron (a solid composed of 20 equilateral triangular faces).

Let's investigate

2 ● Start with a 10 cm × 10 cm square.

● Cut a 1 cm square from each corner.

● Fold up the edges and use the tape to stick the corners to make a box.

a How many 1 cm cubes can you fit in the box?

You need

1 cm squared paper, scissors, sticky tape, centimetre cubes

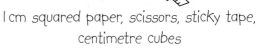
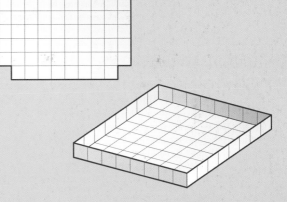

● Now try cutting a 2 cm × 2 cm square from each corner of a 10 × 10 square.

● Make a new box.

b How many 1 cm cubes can you fit in this box?

c Copy the table and record your results.

Starting square	Square cut out of corners	Box dimensions	Number of cubes
10 × 10	1 × 1	8 × 8 × 1	
10 × 10	2 × 2		

d Investigate cutting different sizes of square from the corners.

? What if you started with an 11 cm × 11 cm square?
Which size of box will hold the most cubes?

Let's practise

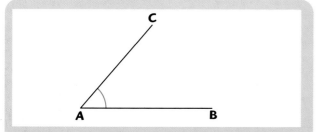

We write angle BAC as: ∠BAC or BÂC or ∠A.
A is the vertex of the angle.
AB and AC are its 'arms'.

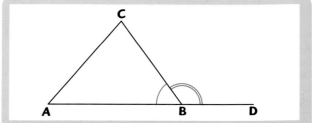

We write triangle ABC as △ABC.
∠ABC is an inside angle of △ABC.
∠CBD is an outside angle of △ABC.

1 **a** Name 3 angles that have AD as an 'arm'.

     b Name 3 angles that have the vertex C.

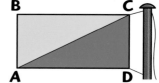

2 **a**

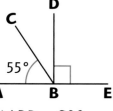

∠ABD = 90°
Calculate ∠DBE
           ∠DBC
           ∠EBC.

b

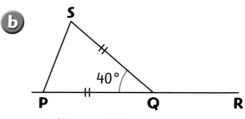

∠PQR = 180°
Calculate ∠SQR
△PQS is isosceles.
Calculate ∠QSP and ∠SPQ.

Let's solve problems

3 ABC is a straight line.
Pairs of equal angles are marked.
Calculate ∠EBH.

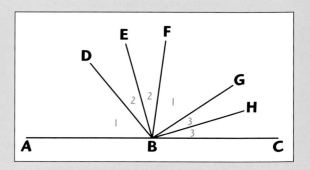

4 You can fit:

- 2 acute angles into a right angle
- 2 acute angles into an obtuse angle
- 2 obtuse angles into a reflex angle
- 3 acute angles into a reflex angle.

     a Copy each statement.
                   b Draw a diagram to test each one.

Let's practise

① Follow the instructions below to draw a triangle.
You are told the length of 2 sides and the angle between them.

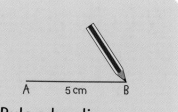

Rule a baseline
AB 5 cm long.

Place the centre of the
protractor over B.

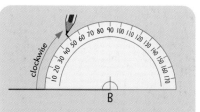

Measure and mark a
clockwise angle of 50°.

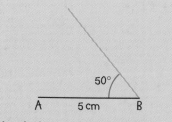

Lightly rule a line to
join the mark to B.
Label the angle.

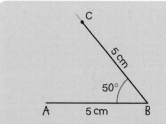

Measure and mark point
C, 5 cm from B.

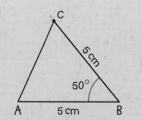

Rule lines to join C to B
and C to A.

Use your ruler and protractor to construct these triangles.

a △ABC with AB = 6·5 cm, AC = 7·5 cm and ∠CAB = 45°

b △DEF with DE = 8 cm, DF = 4·5 cm and ∠FDE = 56°

c △ABC with AB = 3·5 cm, BC = 5·5 cm and ∠CBA = 75°

d △DEF with DE = 7·7 cm, EF = 7·7 cm and ∠DEF = 130°

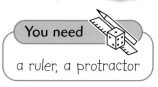

Leonhard Euler (1707–1783)

Euler was the first to use letters *a*, *b* and *c* to indicate the sides of a triangle, and A, B and C for the opposite angles.

Let's investigate

② Draw the triangles, labelling the length of the unknown sides and the third angle.

a

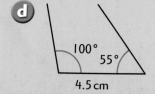

60°   30°

6 cm

b

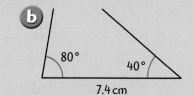

80°   40°

7.4 cm

c

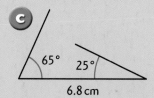

65°   25°

6.8 cm

d

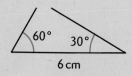

100°   55°

4.5 cm

e

35°   115°

8 cm

f

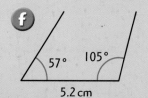

57°   105°

5.2 cm

Let's solve problems

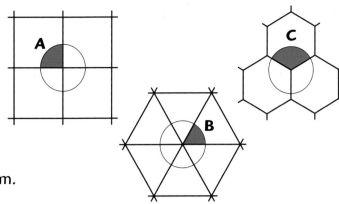

1 Regular tessellations completely fill the space around a point or vertex.

   a Calculate angles A, B and C.

   b Write about how you found them.

2 Semi-regular tessellations use combinations of regular polygons to completely fill the space around a point or vertex.

   a Calculate the size of the marked angles in each tessellation.

   b Write about how you found them.

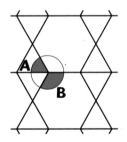
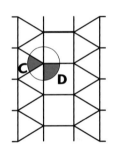
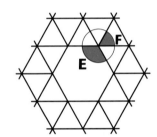
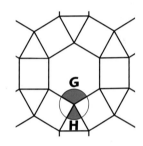

3 Roman mosaics used combinations of regular polygons.

   a Calculate the size of the marked angles.

   b Write about how you found them.

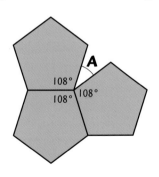
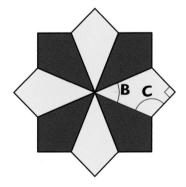
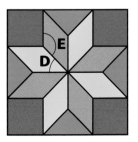
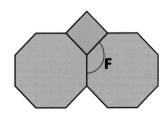

Let's solve problems

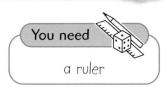

You need

a ruler

The Greek mathematician Thales (c.636 – c.546 BCE), showed the Egyptians how to use the length of a shadow to calculate the height of a pyramid.

He placed a 30 cm stick perpendicular to the ground.

The length of its shadow was 60 cm, twice as long.

At the same time of day, he measured the length of the shadow of the pyramid.

The height of the pyramid must be half the length of its shadow.

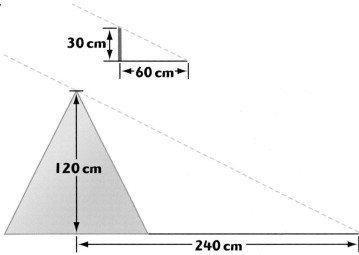

30 cm

60 cm

120 cm

240 cm

1 Find these measurements when the shadow is twice as long as the height.

Length of shadow	50 m		137 m		67·5 m	
Height of pyramid		178 m		209 m		385 m

2 Calculate the height of the obelisk.

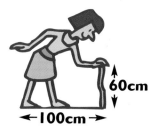

60cm

100cm

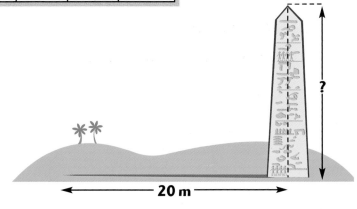

?

20 m

3 The boy is 1·5 m tall and his shadow is 2 m long.
He is standing 6 m away from a date palm.
Find the height of the date palm.

Draw a diagram. Mark all the known lengths.

Let's practise

certain   likely   unlikely   impossible

1 Copy each statement and write the word that best describes it.

   a It will rain tomorrow.

   b Pigs will grow wings and fly.

   c I will walk in space one day.

   d I will be a teacher.

   e I will eat a meal later today.

   f The first person I see tomorrow will be male.

Let's play   A game for 2

You need

a pack of playing cards

- Use only the diamond cards. Shuffle the cards and place them face down.
- Player 1 turns over the top card.
- Player 2 predicts whether the next card will be higher or lower than the previous card.
- Player 1 scores a point for each correct prediction.
- When the prediction is wrong, players swap roles.
- When all the cards have been turned over, the player with more points wins the round.
- Play the game 3 times.

Repeat the game with each player recording the number as a card is turned over.

- How can recording the cards help you make your next prediction?

Prediction	Number
lower	3
higher	2

- Are there any other things that helped you decide whether the next card was likely to be higher or lower?

? What if the game was played using:

   ● 2 suits of cards   ● 3 suits of cards   ● a full pack?

   Does the probability of the next card being higher or lower change?

Let's practise

1 Helen shuffled a suit of playing cards without the picture cards.
She placed them face down in a pile, then turned over the top card.

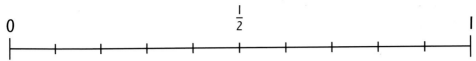

Copy the probability scale.

Record each probability as a fraction on the
probability scale.

a The top card is an ace.

b The top card is an even number.

c The top card is more than 4.

d The top card is less than 9.

e The top card is a multiple of 4.

Let's investigate

2 a Find and record how many children in your classroom:

- there are altogether
- wear glasses
- have blue eyes
- have lace-up shoes
- are female.

b Imagine a giant puts their
hand through the window
and pulls out a child!
Use your results in **a** to work
out the probability of the
giant pulling out a child who:

- wears glasses
- has blue eyes
- has lace-up shoes
- is female.

Let's practise

1 **a** Write all 10 possible additions of 2 of these numbers.

    100   **101**   **102**   **103**   **104**

Calculate the answers.

b Explain why some answers occur more frequently than others.

c Write as a decimal the probability of choosing 2 numbers at random with a sum of: 201, 202, 203, 204, 205, 206, 207.

> ### Probability theory
>
> Blaise Pascal (1623–1662) began investigating probability along with his French countryman Pierre de Fermat (1601–1665).
>
> The first problem he addressed was gambling: his friends had been losing money and wanted to know if there was a way to ensure they won more.
>
> This was the starting point in developing a probability theory.

Let's investigate

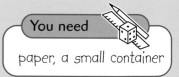

You need

paper, a small container

2 **a** • Write the names of 5 of your friends on pieces of paper.

| Natalie | Lindsey | Ben | Lucy | Ali |

• Think of a name. Write as a decimal the probability that the first piece of paper you take out of a container has that name written on it.

b How many times do you expect each name to appear in 30 selections?

c Put the names in a container and shake it.

• Take out a piece of paper.

• Record the name, replace the paper and shake the container again.

• Do this 30 times altogether.

d Does this agree with your predictions? Explain what you have found.

? What if you took 2, 3, 4 or 5 pieces of paper out at the same time?

How many times would you expect each name to appear?
Give a reason for your answers.

Let's practise

1 Write each number as a decimal fraction of 40 to 2 decimal places.

a 4   **b** 16   **c** 22   **d** 29

e 36   **f** 27   **g** 5   **h** 3

$$\frac{20}{40} = 0.5$$

Let's investigate

You need

a plastic cup or similar

2 When dropped, the cup can land in 3 different ways:

• on its closed end   • on its side   • on its open end

• Hold the top of the cup.
• Drop it from the same height 40 times.
• Record the results in a table.

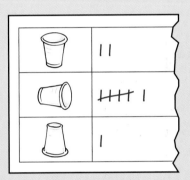

• Use your results to calculate and record the experimental probability of your cup landing on:

a its closed end   **b** its open end

c either end   **d** its side.

• Compare your results with a partner.

e Add your results.
  Use the totals to calculate the experimental probabilities again.

f Are they the same as your individual experimental probabilities?
  Explain what happened.

Tally marks

Archaeologists have found examples of tally marks used by many early cultures. Bones marked with notches have been found in Central Europe and date back to 8500 BCE.

? What if you dropped the cup another 20 times?

Let's practise

1 Work with a partner.

a Predict how many times in
1 minute you think you can say:

- your first name
- your full name
- your name and address
- the name of your school
- your teacher's name.

Ahmed,
Ahmed...

b Write about how you decided.

c Find out and record how many times you can say each in 1 minute.

d Write about the similarities and differences between your predictions
and what you actually managed to do.

Let's investigate

2 Work with a partner.
Simon wonders:

What is the fastest anyone can
read aloud and be understood?

Investigate Simon's question.
Decide, explain why and record:

- how many people you will test
- how long you will test them for
- what you will ask them to read
- how you will record the results
- how you can represent the results.

Now carry out the investigation
and write a report of your findings.

? What if you used a more difficult text?
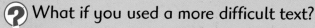

Let's solve problems

1 Work with a partner.
For each of the boxed questions below, discuss, decide and explain:

- what information you would need to collect
- where or who you would collect it from
- how you would collect it.

> **What is the most popular TV programme in the school?**

> **What do you eat for breakfast?**

> **Who is the most popular author for Year 6 children?**

> **Do more people own cats than dogs?**

Let's investigate

2 Work with a partner.
Choose 1 of the boxed questions above.

- Collect the information.
- Represent the data to show the results.
- Write a report of your findings.

Breakfast	Tally
Cereal	
Toast	

Population censuses

One of the biggest forms of data collection is the population census. Many countries carry out a census, usually every 10 years, and record information about the people living there, including their age, members of their family, occupation, and much more. Britain conducted its first official census in 1801.

Let's practise

1 Put each range of numbers into 5 equal-sized groups.

a 1 – 150   **b** 1 – 100   **c** 1 – 60

d 1 – 250   **e** 300 – 349   **f** 0 – 24

50 – 99: ⟶
50 – 59
60 – 69
70 – 79
80 – 89
90 – 99

Let's solve problems

2 These are the results of a test taken in a Year 6 class.

26	25	6	27	30	19
30	20	10	12	29	29
18	20	9	28	18	23
17	19	14	29	17	21
14	30	18	14	26	15

a Group the data and record it in a table.

b Write about what the data tell you.

c Group the data differently to make the results look better.

d Group the data differently to make the results look worse.

Let's investigate

3 a Investigate how many children are in each class in your school.

Would it be helpful to group the data? Explain why or why not.

b What other information about the children in your school could be grouped?

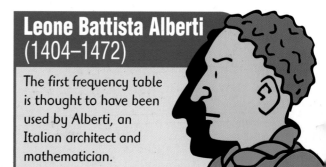

Leone Battista Alberti (1404–1472)

The first frequency table is thought to have been used by Alberti, an Italian architect and mathematician.

Let's practise

1 Record an estimate of:

a the number of trees you can see from your classroom

b the number of baked beans in a tin

c the number of felt tips in your classroom

d the number of children in your school.

Compare your estimates with those of a partner.

Let's investigate

2 Work with a partner.
Which do you think are the busiest areas of your school playground?
Why do you think this is?

> You could work with some friends and each observe a different area of the playground.

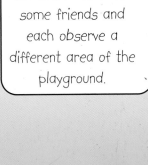

- Decide how to collect evidence to show that you are right (or wrong)!

- Design a data collection sheet.

- At a playtime collect and record your information.

- Write a short report of your investigation. Were you right or wrong about the busiest parts of the playground?

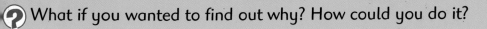

? What if you wanted to find out why? How could you do it?

Let's practise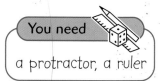

> 100 is 25% of 400

① Write the following numbers as a percentage of 400.

a 200   **b** 50   **c** 300   **d** 40

e 80   **f** 240   **g** 320   **h** 150

Let's solve problems

> **You need**
> a protractor, a ruler

② This is the lunch menu for Mondays at Hill School.

MAIN COURSE
Meatballs in Tomato Sauce
or Cheesy Pizza
or Turkey Burger
Side dish
Potato Wedges
or Slice of Bread
or Salad
or Baked Beans

DESSERT
Fruit Scone
or Chocolate Crispy
or Fruit Pot

The pie charts show the proportions of children who chose each main course and each side dish.

Main course

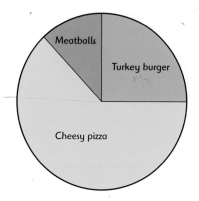

Side dish

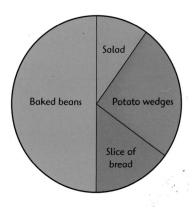

a There are 180 children in the school. Estimate and record the number of children who chose each main course and each side dish.

b Everyone had dessert.
These are the numbers of children who chose each dessert.

Fruit Scone	90
Chocolate Crispy	70
Fruit Pot	20

Construct a pie chart to show this information.

③ Do the children at this school choose healthy lunches?
Explain your reasoning.

Let's practise

1 Calculate and record the median and the range of each set of data.

a 38 17 46 89 20

b 263 260 268 258

c £40 £20 £30 £20 £50

d 5·3 2·8 6·4 4·7 2·8 9·1

e 73 48 74 85 102 56

f 5 17 106 23 211 14 19 48

Let's investigate

You need

coloured counters,
1 metre stick,
10 straws

2 Work with a partner.

a Use a coloured counter and a straw.

- Find out how far each of you can blow the counter with 1 puff through the straw. Now blow without the straw. Do this 3 times each, recording the measurements in a table.

- Ask 8 more people to do the same and record their results.

Name	1st try		2nd try		3rd try	
	With straw	Without straw	With straw	Without straw	With straw	Without straw

b Find the range of each set of data (with straw and without straw).

c Find the median of each set of data.

d What do the range and median tell you about blowing with or without a straw?
- Is it easier to move the counter by blowing through a straw?
- Is it more predictable?

e Write a short report of your investigation.

Let's investigate

Work with a partner.

1 Decide who will check the first 100 words in the
reading book, and who will do the same for the magazine.
Copy and complete the table with your results.

Number of letters in a word	Tally	Frequency
1		
2		
3		

(a) Which word was:
- the longest
- the shortest?

(b) What is the range of the number of letters
in a word?

(c) Use a calculator to help you find the mean
number of letters in a word.

(d) Which number of letters in a word is the mode?

(e) Show how to find the median number of letters in a word.

Remember: to find the
mean, calculate the total
number of letters in all the
words and divide by the
number of words (100).

2 **(a)** Compare the book and magazine results.

(b) Discuss your comparisons.
- Do you think one is easier to read than the other?
  Give a reason for your answer.
- What information helped
  you to decide?

(c) Write a short report of
your investigation.

? What if you compared texts
in 2 different newspapers?